KT-478-630

DISPOSED OF
BY LIBRARY
HOUSE OF LORDS

Jeremy Seabrook was born in Northampton in the Midlands in 1939. He was educated at Northampton Grammar School and Cambridge University before going on to work as a teacher and a social worker. He has written for *New Society* for the last twenty years and now lives and works as a full-time writer. He has explored the themes of poverty and community in many books, including *The Unprivileged*, *What Went Wrong*, *Unemployment* and *Working-Class Children*.

DISPOSED OF
BY LIBRARY
HOUSE OF LORDS

Jeremy Seabrook

The idea of neighbourhood

What local politics should be about

Pluto Press

London and Sydney

First published in 1984 by Pluto Press Limited,
The Works, 105a Torriano Avenue, London NW5 2RX
and Pluto Press Australia Limited, PO Box 199, Leichhardt,
New South Wales 2040, Australia

Copyright © Jeremy Seabrook, 1984

Cover designed by Michael Mayhew

Photoset by A.K.M. Associates (U.K.) Ltd.,
Ajmal House, Hayes Road, Southall, Greater London.
Printed in Great Britain by Photobooks (Bristol) Ltd.
Bound by W.H. Ware & Sons Ltd.
Tweed Road, Clevedon, Avon

British Library Cataloguing in Publication Data

Seabrook, Jeremy
    The idea of neighbourhood.
    1. Citizen's associations — England — Case studies
    2. Community organization — England — Case studies
    I. Title
361.8'0942   JS3251

ISBN 0-86104-768-0

One thing ought to be aimed at by all men: that the interests of each individually, and all collectively, should be the same; for if each should grasp at his individual interest, all human society will be dissolved.

— Cicero

Contents

Acknowledgements

This book is a celebration of one of the bravest initiatives to have been undertaken by any local authority in Britain in recent years. It would not have been possible without the help and support of many people in Walsall. In particular I should like to express my warmest thanks to Brian Powell, Liz Powell and the family; to Dave Church, Steve Johnson, Barrie Blower, and especially Alan Paddock; and to all the neighbourhood officers, staff, workers and people on the estates I visited.

Two pieces – 'The British-birds Man' and part of the Goscote chapter – have appeared in *New Society*; permission to reprint them here is gratefully acknowledged.

Jeremy Seabrook

1. Introduction

> Professional qualifications – housing, social services, whatever –
> remove the professionals from the people. The abstraction of a
> career, geared to a national structure, absorbs people's energy,
> ambition. Those things undermine real commitment to one
> place. They're trained to look on me as a tenant or a client,
> subordinate status. You're not a human being any more, you're
> housing-list applicants waiting for units of accommodation.
>   — Dave Church, former Chairman of Housing

In the last few years the idea of decentralization has become a
source of hope and renewal to many local authorities who felt
themselves becoming more and more remote from the people they
serve. This movement away from centralized bureaucracy has
happened in spite of – or perhaps because of – the fact that the
Conservative government has been undermining local power by its
restrictions and limits on local authority spending and by its
threat to abolish those it sees as the worst offenders – thereby
usurping what many of us has thought was the role of the
electorate.

And yet it isn't difficult to find Conservatives who are in favour
of decentralization, as a means of using limited resources more
efficiently. Liberals, of course, whose community politics through
the 1970s did so much to revitalize the Liberal Party, see it as a way
of humanizing the system, of listening to and taking account of the
feelings of people in the neighbourhoods. Indeed, the Liberals

were the first to show an interest in those daily concerns, which many local councillors, Labour and Conservative, had previously regarded as too trivial or beneath their dignity – the state of the pavements, erratic services, delays in getting minor repairs carried out. It almost began to look as though the Labour Party were going to be left behind in the rush towards the cultivation of the local and the parochial.

But certain initiatives taken by a handful of Labour councils since the late 1970s have opened up the scope and range of what had been seen as an administrative convenience. The most spectacular and far-reaching of these was undoubtedly the opening in 1980 of 33 Neighbourhood Offices in Walsall in the West Midlands, a borough of just over a quarter of a million people. If their principal function has been to deliver an improved housing service, this is because Labour lost control in May 1982 and was prevented from expanding and developing them as a focus for the renewal of communities, many of which had fallen into the decay and neglect of long-term indifference.

Even so, the improvement in the service to the 42,000 council tenants and their families has been dramatic enough. Each office is staffed by people whose appointment depends upon their sympathetic understanding of the lives and problems of the people they serve, and every office is equipped with visual display units which are linked to a central computer. The technology is used not to store away information remote from the people, but in order to give access to those who are on council waiting lists, those needing repairs or asking for transfers to the precise information about where they stand.

The neighbourhoods were defined by the people who live there and have nothing to do with ward boundaries or parish limits or any other imposed administrative conveniences. People always know where their own neighbourhood ceases – at a main road, a canal, a row of shops, a park, a landmark. A neighbourhood is an area where the majority of people know by sight most of those who live there and probably recognize everyone of their own age group; know all the significant buildings and the central focus of the area – shops, schools, libraries, children's playgrounds, clinics, surgeries, youth clubs, Bingo halls, pubs, or whatever.

It is not by chance that the initiative should have come from this part of the West Midlands. Walsall is, in fact, a series of small towns and industrial villages, which grew throughout the nineteenth century out of migrants from Wales and Ireland and the surrounding countryside who came to work in the foundries and small metal, leather and engineering works, the manufacture of locks, chains, nails, hinges. Traces of these earlier communities still remain. Many of the old Victorian cottages still have a workshop in the back yard, often now in ruins or converted into garages; there are still faded notices on blank brick walls announcing the long-defunct services of farriers or harness-makers. There has always been a strong sense of regional identity which, under the influence of all the centralizing tendencies in modern life – whether government bureaucracies or multinational companies – was bound sooner or later to reassert itself. Partly, this is a reaction against all those influences which seem to diminish the local, usurp regional autonomy, plugging the whole population into a uniform and media-created public spectacle, in which the local is dwarfed (so that what passes for regional news on TV consists of a murder in Birmingham, a visit of a member of the royal family to open a building and the weather forecast – a barren unimaginative account of what a region is). It has come to seem as if all the important decisions that touch our lives are made elsewhere, by someone else, someone distant and unidentified; and that we are shaped by great economic and social forces barely within the control of human agencies at all. The effect of this has been to create a widespread feeling of impotence, especially on the part of those who have the roughest deal in society – 'What can you do about it?' 'What's the point?' 'Who's going to take any notice of us?' This in turn leads to a total disbelief in those who claim that they can do anything about it – and that means, for the most part, politicians.

This more radical undertaking which Walsall began in 1980 hits at the heart of even more destructive tendency in contemporary life – one that has been monitored for many years: a certain retreat from community, the faltering, in large sections of the working class, of commitment to collective values, the withering, not of the outer forms, but of the very roots of solidarity itself. These things were always the motive and driving force of working-class institutions, the Labour Party and the trade unions, and formed the human basis for such impulses towards socialism as we have so far seen in this country, whether the growth of Chartism, the great organization of the unskilled workers at the end of the nineteenth century, the General Strike or the election of 1945.

This tendency for ideas of community to be on the defensive isn't something that expresses itself abstractly at the local level. Its symptoms are far more immediate and vivid; many of them are so familiar by now that we have almost ceased to pay any attention to them at all. It is a complaint that has been heard from all over the country, especially in the urban areas and the poorest estates – the sites of those older close-knit working-class communities. There has been a sustained and untiring ideological assault on traditional working-class values, initiated and egged on by the media, with its shifting focus on threats and fears that undermine community – all the scares about mugging, or rapists or vandals; the scare about scroungers and idlers, the hysteria about aliens and migrants, the panic about child-molesters, drug addicts or alkies, glue-sniffers, hooligans, criminals, moles, Reds and wreckers – have swept regularly through the working-class districts. Whatever the resilience, they do, in the end, have some effect. Local newspapers are always full of stories about the rape of old women, the knifings after a party, drug-and-sex orgies behind the façade of an ordinary council house, callous and brutal robberies; and if this weren't enough, it has been supported by a sustained diet from what is grotesquely miscalled the entertainment industry – films and videos and TV series which seemed designed to show us all the horrors and cruelties that human beings are capable of. For more than a generation we have been subjected to the mocking and cynical message that you can't trust anyone any more. We have been slow to recognize this for the ideological assault it is and that it originates with those who have an interest in dissolving the old industrial communities, out of which the great potential for change in the labour movement grew, and which seemed to be on the edge of such spectacular success even as recently as 1945.

It is for these reasons that a project that bases itself on the reality of neighbourhood in the 1980s is actually engaged in one of the great ideological battles of our time. It cannot help asking questions that have not been asked on the left for many years. It soon finds itself caught up in the fight back against the break in the post-war settlement which happened with the coming to power of Margaret Thatcher in 1979 and her triumphant inroads into those gains and improvements which we, on the left, had serenely believed to have won for ever.

The Walsall initiative has required courage and imagination – qualities that have not been prominent in local politics in recent years. The capacity to hold on to a vision, the clear-sighted anticipation of all the difficulties, the skill and commitment of those who supported the initiative – all these things were needed to get the scheme going. The Labour leadership knew that there would be resistance from various council departments. They knew that the professional advice and judgements of the officers might have to be overridden. They had to resolve not to be deterred by all the obstacles that expertise and specialization might devise. In order for the dream to become council policy, it would have to be implemented quickly; and that is why within less than 18 months, 33 Neighbourhood Offices were open and functioning. When the Conservative-Liberal 'anti-socialist coalition' of May 1982 was formed, the neighbourhood idea was sufficiently well established to rule out closure as a serious option, in spite of all the criticism and obstruction of the changed administration.

In the following chapters I shall look at the kind of problems which the neighbourhoods reveal, through an account of some time I spent in one of the largest and poorest estates in the town; then a look at the way in which the scheme has helped to transform what was a demoralized slum area. Next is an attempt to reveal the real strengths and resistances, the untapped talents which so many working-class people still offer and without which any neighbourhood idea would end up as nothing more than a hollow organizational shell. There follows an account of the origin and development of the idea from the beginnings of the inner-area

Caldmore Advice Centre to the initiative of the 1980s. There is a chapter on the response of the media to the project, and the attempt to misrepresent its intention. Finally, I shall try to place the enterprise in context and assess its importance to the wider labour movement.

2. Living in the neighbourhood

A poor estate, in Walsall. Some of the houses in bad condition; even so most of them are well maintained, the gardens tended. One house on the corner looks conspicuously run-down: all the windows are broken, the curtains are flapping through the jagged glass; the privet hedge grown out of control. 'Is that one empty?' I ask two women talking in the road. 'Oh no. The man who lives there is a bit funny. He gets his windows broken by the kids. They like to play him up.' They return to their conversation.

It is a mistake to think of council estates as being monolithic and uniform provision for only one sort of people. Tony Parker, in his book *The People of Providence*, has shown the variety and range of people to be found on one estate in south London. In most provincial towns, each council estate has a distinctive atmosphere: they embody the social history of the period at which they were built. In this way, each estate has its own flavour, its own characteristics that distinguish it from later or earlier ones. For instance, the first estates – and the pattern in Walsall is that of most middle-sized industrial centres – were almost always of red brick, semi-detached, with narrow streets just wide enough for the milk-cart, the coalwaggon, the hearse, and certainly not designed to accommodate private cars. They have decent-sized gardens, but the houses offered only rudimentary comfort – a draughty lavatory in the porch, a bathtub, sometimes occupying a corner of the kitchen, open fires, but no heating in the bedrooms.

They were built at a time when it would have been felt improper to pamper the working class with too many amenities. These estates sheltered some of the worst-housed people in the period after the First World War; and in them you still find the essence of the old provincial community, the strongest local accent, the people who worked in the traditional industries that were the mainstay of the town. For the most part, the people came from overcrowded privately rented slums in the heart of the old town; in Walsall, many of the early council dwellers were living in shacks and courts in the town centre. Because these were some of the earliest public housing, they have now decayed. Those who lived there originally have died; either their children have taken over the tenancy or people have been housed there who, it was felt, did not require particularly high standards. In other words, some of them became dumping-grounds for some of the most vulnerable families, those with multiple difficulties. These are the estates where the gardens fill with rubbish, the potholes in the road get bigger, the kerbs crumble, the privet runs out of control and the dogs roam in packs. The houses get boarded up, the already scant amenities deteriorate, the phones never work, the shops are reduced to betting-shop, an ill-stocked and expensive mini-supermarket with rusty grilles at the window, a sweet shop and tobacconist's – or, worse still, a mobile shop that visits only twice a week. What can be done with one of these estates will be looked at in the next chapter, the renewal of the Gostcote area of Walsall.

Many of the estates built through the 1930s are similar. Many of them were of course constructed on poor sites, where private builders were reluctant to speculate, because they knew they would never sell the houses. This means that such estates are often in a dingy environment, close to industrial areas, in the shadow of foundries, mills or railway sidings; or else they sprawl on the edge of town, with poor bus services; petering out in fields of rough pasture where horses or sheep browse and where the canal floods in winter. Again, most of the original inhabitants of these houses will have been those from overcrowded slum areas. Many will have died by now. Some of their children still live there – the conservatism of the poorer working class is a powerful factor in tying people to the districts that are familiar. But there was still a powerful sense of community – people tended to work in the same places, to have retained the same expectations – (that is, very modest ones); only there was more scope for keeping pigeons, growing vegetables, keeping hens and rabbits in the gardens. Many of these houses are reaching the stage where complete renewal is necessary. Some councils have completely modernized these estates and, where this has happened, the purchase of these houses by the sitting tenants is a quite attractive proposition. But because they were often built on poor land, some have severe structural problems. The Delves estate in Walsall was built on old mineworkings. Here, subsidence has caused the walls to buckle and cracks to appear – some of which are so wide that you can actually reach into the next room through them. The floors slope, windows are stuck in their frames, gaps show under the door.

The estates built after the Second World War probably house a far wider range of people than any have done, either before or since. After the war, the great extension of home ownership was not immediately foreseen. Many people who had suffered bomb damage, or who had just come out of the army, and who had previously lived in poor conditions, saw their only hope as a new council house. With the 1945 Labour government, and the promise it held, it seemed that council housing, the new towns, were to be a major initiative in public provision. There was certainly no question of any stigma in being a council tenant. And indeed, the planning and siting of the post-war estates and the new towns provided some of the best housing ever undertaken by local authorities. Generously proportioned estates grew up on the edge of towns, space was not stinted, the sites were landscaped and well provided with trees and open spaces. Roads on these estates form great sweeping curves and it is possible to walk half a mile and pass no more than 25 or 30 houses, with ample greens in front of them. These are the houses that have been most widely bought by sitting tenants under the Conservatives' house-selling policy; and they constitute some of the most desirable public housing stock. There is not the same pressure on people in these estates to get out into private estates, as has occurred in many of the public house-building projects that have been built since. These were the former Labour strongholds, which were so vulnerable to the swing to the Conservatives at the elections of 1979 and 1983. They have a stability and community sense that has evaded many later housing schemes.

It wasn't until the later 1950s that high-rise estates appeared, with their tower blocks which re-housed people from the wasting streets of the central areas, streets that were characteristic of the mid-nineteenth century, and from which by no means everybody was eager to move at the time of the great slum clearances of the late 1950s and 1960s. When tower blocks were first built, they were heralded as the last word in modernism and excitement. I can recall when the first 10-storey block was planned in my home town, Northampton. It was hailed in the local paper 'Manhattan Comes to Northampton' and people clamoured to live there. It was only later that some of the defects became obvious; even though, it has to be said, tower blocks have been blamed for other processes that are also at work in society – that loss of cohesion and sense of place that has been a feature of so many towns and cities. And it wasn't until the later 1950s that the more prosperous and secure sections of the working class began to buy their own houses on a large scale. This had always happened to some extent but it intensified in the period around 1960. The formerly genteel areas of town – bay-windowed villas that had formerly accommodated the Edwardian lower-middle class – became the homes of working people, as well as the better working-class streets. By this time, the movement away from the traditional working-class communities was well under way.

One consequence of this was that, as the 1960s went on and the large-scale redevelopments were undertaken, there was a narrower band of people being re-housed by the council. That is to say, principally those who had little hope of buying a home of their own: the poorest, who never get a mortgage because their income was unreliable or too low, their work intermittent and not secure. Some of these new estates had less of the leaven of the more able and articulate working people, with the result that there was often only a handful of individuals who could speak up for the tenants, and they began to receive an inferior service. This period coincided also with vast debts that some of the poorer councils were incurring in the repayments of interest on loans; and newer, cheaper designs were sought. This deteriorating standard has resulted in certain estates being declared unfit for habitation only 15 years after they were built. The 1960s and early 1970s saw the high-density concrete developments, honeycombs, slabs, monoliths; many of them built with garages beneath which, as the youngsters colonized them, soon became no-go areas covered with graffiti, sites of muggings, drinking and glue-sniffing. The people who lived in these places were well aware that the stigma of being a council tenant was growing – until the majority of the population were home-owners, and they became a minority – and one that was likely to go on decreasing as more and more people bought the council house they occupied. Of course, the vast majority of people even in the worst council housing are good and decent, doing their best to bring up their families in difficult circumstances; but there is a concentration of the weaker and more vulnerable in the poorer areas – single parents, the elderly, the disabled, those with few skills and no ability to increase their earning power, the mentally or emotionally disturbed, the less well endowed. It has been interesting to observe that the departure of many of those who might have been community leaders has weakened the resistance to vandalism, petty crime, the many aggravations of daily life in the poor areas, the growth in some estates where there are a few black people of racism; the threat of violence, the break-up of so many families.

The core of the Blakenall estate was built in the 1930s; added to after the war with some flats and tower blocks that date from the 1960s. Of the 4,271 households in the area, there are 495 owner-occupiers. These are 2,399 council tenants, 82 are privately rented and there are 10 housing association homes. There are 660 single-person households; 84 have seven or more people in them. Old-age pensioners occupy 1,441 of the houses. There are 281 'concealed households' – families, young couples, lodgers waiting to be re-housed. There are 1,072 on the borough waiting list, which stands at 13,996. These figures (1981) do not reveal that there are 203 single-parent families or that the unemployment rate is around 30 per cent. Even less do they give any inkling of the way people see their own problems: the woman, herself elderly, living in terror of what her senile mother would do next and afraid to ask for help because what she dreads most is losing her and being left alone; the teenager who had run away from home, and was living secretly with his mate, creeping into the house only after the family were in bed; the man who said he felt he had been thrown on the scrap-heap and would never work again, and who, at 38, was talking like an old man. I sat one day in the pub with a man who had just come out of prison. He had done 12 months, because he had discovered that his wife had found someone else. 'What did I do? I went home and beat the fuck out of the two kids. They probably weren't mine anyway. Then I went up the school and beat the fuck out the boy. Then I went back and beat the fuck out of her. Then I got in the car and waited for the boyfriend to come out of work and I tried to run the bastard down. And then I beat the fuck out of two coppers.' He had come back to Blakenall, he said, for one reason. 'Revenge. Nothing else would bring me back to a shit-hole like this.'

The estate stretches perhaps half a mile. Towards the main road, the houses are well kept and more attractive, the gardens well tended. But as you penetrate deeper into the area, the neglect becomes more tangible. You can almost locate the very house where the first step of deteriorating property occurs; and then, further on, even the semblance of dignity is abandoned and the streets were an air of long-term neglect and indifference. There is the shell of an abandoned car in a garden, rusty and broken; in another, a sodden armchair of crimson moquette, a stained mattress soaked with rain, some scrap metal. A deserted workshop displays parts of engines, batteries, oily patches on the concrete. There is a goat in one garden, in another a horse is tethered. Some hens peck at the sour overgrown grass on the verge. A row of old people's bungalows – with Jacobean-style gables, a bit after the design of alms-houses – has been boarded up; the doors have been removed, the windows smashed, they are surrounded by a wire fence. The old people had to be moved out for their own safety, because of the danger of being robbed or attacked. Further still, there is a block of grey flats constructed in the 1960s; four storeys high, concrete cubes, with short gardens in front and a piece of waste ground behind. From some of them pipes and fittings have been removed, floorboards taken for firewood. All around splinters of glass, wood, bottles, cans, paper, some rank, faded grass smelling of cats. Some windows have the marks of airgun pellets which have passed through without shattering. Those that are still occupied have pieces of cardboard or wallpaper blocking the broken windows. In some of the rooms you can see a plastic chandelier, a torn plastic sofa, a bare light-bulb on a flex, a dartboard, a bird cage, some pictures of pop stars and footballers bleached by the sun, a football scarf.

Parts of the neighbourhood are well maintained; the privet cut back, the houses well furnished; but even there the pavements are crumbling, the street-lights smashed, the bus shelter vandalised. Here poverty eats into people's self-respect. You can see it in the overflowing dustbins, the half-wild scavenging dogs, the anxious mothers and their children eating uneconomic ready-cooked food in the street, the fuel cut-offs, the debt and the arrears, the shabby second-hand clothing, the outdated fashions, the children in skimpy dresses inappropriate for a cold March day. The hardship is tangible; yet, at the same time, so is the acceptance, the patience and docility of the poor. The wonder is not that there is so much crime and vandalism and despair, but that the vast majority of people remain decent and hard-working, striving to do the best for their children in this unpromising place.

In one sense, people don't live in the neighbourhood at all. There they simply exist. The living is done inside – not only inside the houses which, in spite of the shabbiness and the poverty, are for the most part warm and not without comfort, but inside the head, where the fantasies and the images from the media and the television penetrate poorest and well-to-do alike, with their invitations to escape, to dream and to forget. It is those images, those stereotypes of living which come to dominate even the most dispossessed – that constant stream of images of a better world that exists, tantalizingly, hauntingly, just out of reach, but in such close parallel to that worse one which most people here inhabit, that world of unemployment, mislaid giros, junk food, debt, anxiety, mental breakdown, fear of the future, hardship and sickness, the appearance in court and the geriatric ward.

The Neighbourhood Office in Blakenall is a black-painted wooden prefabricated building, with a ramp leading to the reinforced-glass door. It is always crowded. All the encounters described here are the result of listening and talking to the people who bring not only their worries about housing, but also many of the deeper problems that burden them and agitate their lives.

It is only just after nine o'clock, but there is already a queue of people waiting. They stand inside the building on the rubberized floors, looking at the racks of booklets offering to help claimants.

The woman is elderly. She wears a crimson raincoat and a felt hat beaded with rain. She holds her coat before her with her purse in her hand; her skin is dry and grained. She sits on the black plastic chair with the apologetic and uncertain air of that older generation of working people who have never asked anyone for anything. She is due to be re-housed, being the oldest tenant in the block where there are a lot of teenagers. 'We shall have to get out.' Her voice is pleading. 'Can't you gee 'em up a bit? . . . The kids are making our life a misery.' Her husband is in hospital now, having a brain scan. He has been having fits for some time and these have become worse recently. 'The kids do nothing but knock at the window or the door. They've broken the fence down. Every time he hears them, it starts off one of these fits. It's no way to live. I've had a heart attack myself.' She goes on to talk about the indifference of the young to her old age and the fragility of the life of herself and her husband. Her greatest fear is that she will die first and leave him unable to cope. 'I pray God he'll go first,' she says, 'even thought he is my whole life. I'd be nothing without him.' Her attitude towards the young goes from bewilderment to anger. How can they behave so? 'If we'd behaved like that, the grown-ups would have clouted your ear; and it'd be no good going to your mam or dad, they'd give you another one 'cause they knew you deserved whatever you got. One of the mothers, she said to me, "Let them alone, they want to enjoy theirselves." It's their enjoyment, but it's our *life*. My dad would have given me a good hiding right up to the age of 21 ... Once, I'd been to a dance' and as she remembers her eyes glisten; you can see her relax and expand in the feeling that she can talk safely here, 'and my father said, "Be in by ten o'clock." Well, it was half past. And there he stood, at the end of the street waiting for me. With a belt in his hand. I was 19. Could you imagine that today? My dad always used to say, "Hard work, no rest, kills horses, breaks engines." I can hear him saying it.' Her sister, who is mentally handicapped, lives with them. She goes to training centres and she, too, is teased and mocked by the children. When they move, at least her sister will be nearer the training centre. 'I don't know. We don't drink and we don't smoke. What've we done to finish up like this? We've worked all our lives.'

She becomes aware of the queue building up behind her and gets up to go. She is assured that she will be moved within a couple of weeks. It is the policy of the authority to move out old people if they are harassed by the young. Anything to keep things quiet. Nobody has an answer to her question when she asks what kind of a society it is that accepts it as part of the nature of things that the young will so torment the old that they have to be moved out of the district.

As the morning goes on, some of the dark-blue leaflets from the DHSS fall from the rack and are trodden underfoot. Cigarette ends get pressed into the strip of durable carpet, muddy shoeprints form dance patterns on the floor. Waiting time has soon increased to three-quarters of an hour. There are a dozen people now; and there is something familiar, something wrong. It is the eternal waiting of the poor, the resignation, the patience. Mothers with toddlers on reins, a pram that has been wheeled out of the cold, a baby buggy, an unemployed couple, an old man with emphysema, a woman whose legs are so deformed that she can scarcely stand without holding on to her sister. The poor have already learned to wait here, as they wait elsewhere. It is as though every new initiative gets invaded by old familiar patterns. There is never quite enough time to give to each person; and in spite of the sympathetic reception, the friendly response, there remains a painful undertow of dissatisfaction, of something incomplete. This means that even though the practical problems the staff deal with are real enough, they are often only a fraction of deeper wrongs and greater grievances; even though the people themselves are not quite sure how to express them, how to given them voice. What is visible here is the way in which so many of the issues raised – intensely political, many of them – are not seen as part of political debate at all. Why can't the young understand the experience of the old? How can the old people say the young are lucky when they have been brought to a life in which they have no function or purpose? Why do I feel so alone? Why do I need tranquillizers for a life that is so empty? Why do I feel I'm finished when I should be in the prime of life? The political has been diminished, set apart, removed from the deep things of our lives, as though it had nothing to do with 'private' life, that very place where capitalist ideology creates its ravages unresisted. Is it any wonder that people express the same feelings about all politicians, Labour, Conservative alike – they're all the same, they don't care, they're all out for themselves, they all piss in the same pot, they're all out to line their own pockets. All the confusion comes from the way in which the labour movement has accepted the logic and ideology of the system it came into being to fight – that the purpose of working-class struggle is wealth and not emancipation.

The way the people in the room are standing hurts: leaning against the wall, shoulders rounded, hands clasped, arms folded; the lengthening queue is a frieze of figures in attitudes of defeat.

The woman is in her fifties; nervous, with troubled blue eyes and a permanent frown of anxiety. A beige raincoat, knitted woollen gloves clasping and unclasping the handbag in her lap. Her fence needs mending. A car that had been stolen was being pushed up the hill, when it ran out of control and finished up in her garden, breaking the fence and coming to a halt just underneath her window. Now, every time a car comes down the hill, she imagines it is going to burst through the garden, into the front room where she is sitting, wrecking everything. It emerges that her husband is in hospital. No, they don't know what's wrong with him. You can tell from the intensity with which she talks that the broken fence is a metaphor for other anxieties. It looks like a trivial matter – a broken fence, there are hundreds of them on the estate. But what seem like minor matters to officials often have a much greater significance in the lives of the people concerned with them; and they become invested with all sorts of displaced feelings and anxieties. To ignore them or brush them aside is to deny people in a very basic way. The neighbourhood officer understands what she is saying; and he promises to give the repair priority.

A man in his early thirties; well built and smartly dressed in fawn trousers and blue shirt. He doesn't stand in the queue but walks up and down, reading the notices on the wall, looking out of the window, playing with his car keys. He looks self-confident, macho; only the restlessness of his movement betrays the inner anxiety. He has been working as a residential social worker. Now he has been turned out by his wife and is staying with a friend for the time being. He says that being a social worker has ruined his marriage. The job with handicapped children has taken over his life. He says, with an air of renunciation, that it is probably best if he moves out; the continual argument with his wife has been upsetting his children; their behaviour has become disturbed. The prospect of homelessness – bad enough – is actually secondary in his case to his own feelings of guilt. This is what he wants to talk about. Why do so many marriages break down? Why do people's lives fall apart so easily? So many of the people he knows are splitting up. Why are our attachments to each other so fragile, what is it that turns those we love – or thought we loved – into our bitterest enemies? How can it be that this father's highest duty to his children is to abandon them? These are the things that concern him; but they all get smothered by the question of whether he should join the list for single-person accommodation in Walsall. There is very little chance that he will be offered anything. 'What am I supposed to do, then – walk the streets?' In many of these encounters, it is clear that the immediate issue becomes a means of keeping the lid on far graver problems. The existence of the Neighbourhood Offices has encouraged the release of some of these pent-up feelings, these suppressed problems, these discussions that have had no place to be aired, and have been thrust back, unceremoniously, into the private lives of individuals.

A shabby and depressed couple, in their forties. She has a thin pale face, straggly hair and deep marks around her eyes. He is embarrassed and avoids the eyes of those he speaks to. They gave up the tenancy of their flat a year ago and went to lodge with friends, 'or at least we thought they were friends. We know different now.' Now they are homeless. She wears cork-heeled plastic boots that have wrinkled up and collapsed and a dingy leopard-spot plastic coat. He has longish though receding hair, eyes that haven't slept for days; wears a red polo-neck sweater and baggy trousers; there is a growth of several days' silver stubble on his chin. Why did they give up their flat in the first place? They were harassed by their neighbours. Why were they harassed? Because I wasn't working. Half the people in that road aren't working; how could that be it? I'd been in trouble. Who isn't in trouble round there? Perhaps it was because we like a drink.

The story of being persecuted, harassed, pestered, disturbed, molested is one that recurs regularly. There is a constant refrain, not that the system is unjust oppressive and cruel, but that other people are the problem. It is here that the ideology of a lopsided individualism has its darkest consequences; and we can see the imbalance of a society which boasts its concern for the individual, but excludes those needs that are for the fraternal, the collective. In this way, a large part of human need is denied, outlawed; just as in some societies which call themselves socialist, the collective is exalted and the individual needs are crushed and broken.

A man in his early thirties, with short fair hair, blue eyes a defensive and aggressive manner. His wife, pregnant, a few years younger, dark-haired, suede coat, sits beside him and says nothing. She constantly flicks non-existent ash from her cigarette. As he speaks, she casts her eyes down. He has just come out of the army and they are living with her parents in one room of a council house. They already have one child and another is due in a couple of months.

He says, 'I want a house. All the unmarried mothers, all that crap, all the immigrants, all them on welfare sitting on their arses, they get priority. I want a house, and I mean a house. I don't want a slum. I don't want some crappy hole that's full of all the shit and filth of whatever rubbish lived in it before. If I don't get what I want I'm going to squat. I'll force an entry. There's all these houses boarded up. I don't care if I have to go to jail . . . I've done 16 years in the army. The army's like everything else, going down the shoot. Load of cissies and pansies in it. It's like the rest of the country – sinking under all the parasites and scroungers in it. I've given 16 years to my country and now I want somewhere decent to live. I'm living downstairs at her mother's. I'm not having the kiddies brought up like that.'

It is amazing how many young people – in their thirties – have taken up the cry that the country is going downhill, that things are getting worse; a kind of inherited nostalgia, because during their brief lifetime it's impossible that they could have witnessed the sort of decline they say they feel. Steve, the assistant neighbourhood officer, takes the couple over to the visual display unit. The green screen flickers. Steve presses the keys. Their position registers on the screen. They have 437 points. A month ago they had only 350; and yet they have gone down from second to third on the list in the area they have asked for. 'How the fuck can that be? We're worse off, but we've got more points. Jesus wept.' 'Well, it means that somebody has come on to the list who is in a worse position than you are. Maybe someone disabled with a sick child, living in even worse conditions.' They are told that if they're willing to consider other districts of the town, they will almost certainly move into first place, which means that they could move as soon as a property becomes vacant – usually a matter of a few days. The man is obviously reassured by the visual evidence of the priority his situation has been given. He feels a little ashamed of his earlier aggressiveness. This occurs several times a day in most offices. People come in to monitor the change in their position from week to week. When they see that they are making some headway, that they haven't been forgotten, their application hasn't been filed away or lost, they are always much happier.

The man doesn't apologize for his outburst, but you can see he feels slightly guilty; and his wife's downward look is one of shame. There is something very poignant in the machismo of these working-class communities, where the work was such that the hardness and strength of the men was an essential component of back-breaking labour. Now that so much of the heavy manual work has gone, the toughness remains; in some ways, it gets even more hardened, precisely because there is no longer any need for it; an assertiveness and defiance in the face of social and economic change over which people feel they have no control. It is no use ridiculing or shaming that toughness – it will only become more entrenched. There are a lot of men like this in these communities – the display of hardness, bluster and swearing only conceals the trauma of the fact that the hard lifetime of labour for which they were raised is now disappearing and will not return.

A small man, with an expressionless ashen face, sunken eyes, balding. He wears a shabby grey suit, frayed shirt, shoes that are coming apart. Last night, a brick came through the window of his house. Tonight he has been promised a petrol bomb. He knows who is responsible, but he daren't tell anyone for fear of what will happen to him. He says it would be more than his life is worth to tell the police. In some areas the fear of reprisals is stronger than trust in the police to do anything. The only answer is to get out. It's all done through the kids of his enemies, he says. The kids are out of control. His talk suggests imminent catastrophe. Everything is going to the dogs. He feels he is cracking up. He hasn't worked for 18 months, when the foundry where he worked for 14 years closed down. He is one of those people who shrink with unemployment; his very weakness invites bullying and persecution. There is also something comforting in the assault of violent neighbours: at least you can make sense of that; it is far easier to deal with than the vast impersonal forces that throw you out of work, destroy your sense of self, wreck your life in ways that seem arbitrary and incomprehensible. The malice of neighbours – that's something you can understand. This is, of course, one of the great strengths of capitalism. Because of the diffuse and remote nature of its structures, its spread halfway across the world, it is difficult for people at the local level to see its workings. That is one of the reasons why the poor turn on each other; and that's what makes the reconstitution of solidarity such a vital and yet difficult task.

'Will you get me out of that place?' His priority for moving is not high. It isn't easy to bend the points system in such a way that a vulnerable personality can be taken account of. He says bitterly, 'If I do away with meself, will you move me then – or just leave me to rot?'

A young couple; she is about 18, he perhaps a year older. The girl is eight months' pregnant, pale anaemic face, downward curve of the lips. The young man has been sacked from his labouring job for something still described in the DHSS manuals as 'industrial misconduct'. This means that for six weeks he will receive no unemployment benefit. They have just had notice of action to be taken over the arrears of rent that have mounted up – just over £400. They had saved up their money to get married; the baby is due within two or three weeks. They feel they couldn't not get married for the baby's sake: 'You've got to give it a name.' But it means that the rent has been sacrificed: 'You've got to have a proper wedding.' The need for ceremonial in a society which has dispensed with all festivals except those that can be harnessed for profit leaves people with the need to create their own celebrations: something to mark the important events in life, to show the world that you do count for something, even though there is little enough recognition of it. To splash out all the money you have on a big wedding is an attempt to retrieve something personal from a depersonalized indifferent society. Their wedding was an assertion of the human. To say that they should have spent their money on rent is an insult to the importance of the event that has occurred in their lives. And yet they are made to feel ashamed and furtive, as though daring to give expression to their relationship, celebrating their love for each other were to rob the state.

A woman in her forties, dark hair in tight curls, anxious and depressed; she clasps and unclasps her handbag as she speaks. She is a widow with three children, the oldest 14. She wants to move from the area. The boy of 14 has become involved with glue-sniffers. They go into one of the disused flats; they have prised the wood from the doorway and made a secret hideaway for themselves, replacing the wood over the door when they leave it, even nailing it back in place. One morning she went over there and found plastic bags, glue-containers, empty beer cans and even bottles of whisky and vodka. She says his behaviour has changed over the past few months. 'He gets all moody, he's got such a temper. All he wants is money. He's not my son any more – I hardly recognize him. It's these older boys he's mixed up with. I know it's not having a father. He takes it out on me and his sisters. I didn't ask to be left a widow. He threatens me. He says he'll break everything up in the house if I don't give him money. I've got to get away. I feel we must get away, make a fresh start somewhere else.'

People's lives seem to overflow here: a spillage of pain and anxiety and, above all, their lack of power to cope with the things that trouble them. They feel they are on their own with their fears; 'I can't cope,' 'I don't know which way to turn,' are recurring themes.

It is one of the great ironies that those values which the best of the working class forged in opposition to the poverty and insecurity of capitalism – the mutuality and the sharing, the sense of a collective predicament, the imaginative understanding of other people's suffering – were precisely those which shaped the idea of the welfare state. It looked as if those very things which working people had created to mitigate some of the harshness of life were going to be vested in the structures of society itself. The welfare state looked to many working people as the public acknowledgement of things they had always known: that security, care and comfort must be given unstintingly to those in need. It seemed as though that unofficial and unsung ability to care for each other had come to a wider recognition at last: enshrined in the institutions and statutes of the land.

Forty years later, it doesn't look quite like that. We can see now what happens to socialist ideas when they are launched into a capitalist context; how they become subtly deformed and debased. None of those old labour idealists who worked so selflessly for the realization of that vision of the welfare state could have imagined that it would involve the abandonment of care and concern within the communities themselves. It was seen as an extension of that caring, a relief from some of the most heroic sacrifices that women in particular had made. But to some extent, those values have been expropriated, drained out of the communities and become frozen in cumbersome, bureaucratic and indifferent structures. Of course, the numberless acts of kindness and charity that individuals perform for each other every day form an oasis of light and comfort; but personal goodness cannot transcend the values of the society and there is no substitute for solidarity.

The welfare state seemed to deliver us from unemployment, destitution, hunger, anxiety about health for the first time. In the process, it prepared us for that transformation of capitalism that came to be known as the age of affluence, the consumer society. In other words, the achievements of the labour movement were actually used in order that capitalism could be reconstructed and strengthened in such a way that the resistances and defences of the working class would be weakened. It looked for decades as though capitalism had changed and the sacrifices that were demanded of the working class looked quite acceptable — the breaking of solidarity, the disintegration of communities, the destruction of some of the old strengths and resistances in the name of redevelopment, modernization, improvements, rationalization. But it has all tended towards the same long-term result, to undermine, disarm the working class, so that the old barbarities and cruelties can be imposed all over again – mass unemployment, poverty and the threat of war. The circle is almost complete. All those things to which a generation after 1945 said, 'Never again,' are beginning to re-emerge; and they find the labour movement uncertain, divided.

Throughout the day in Blakenall, the queue doesn't diminish; only in the middle of the day, there is a respite of perhaps half an hour. Before two o'clock there is a growing crowd of people standing in the rain.

A young couple, neither more than 18. She has a beautifully sensitive face; a gold cross in her ear, auburn hair. She is wearing an imitation suede coat. (So many of the poor people wear things that are counterfeit, imitation of the dress of the rich – simulated leather, false furs, bogus silk, imitation gold, copies of jewels and precious stones. It all suggests so many forgotten or submerged questions – whether real gold, real furs and real jewels should be the object of the working-class struggle; or whether our own values and ideals should be forged in opposition to these things; and what room is there for socialist visions in the face of the gaudy, showy counterfeits of the capitalist market-place.) The boy is not wearing a coat in spite of the cold; he prefers to leave his arms bare, with their fresh tattoos, a snake and a tombstone in blue and red, LOVE and HATE on the knuckles; a swallow at the throat and a tattoo that reads '99 per cent sex'. Pete and Linda are living with Linda's sister. Pete doesn't get on with the sister's bloke and they are always fighting. All of them are out of work; in the long empty days, jealousies, rivalries flare up suddenly, without warning. Pete says the other guy is jealous of him and Linda. He is trying to make it with her. Last night there was a big argument and Pete was turned out. Linda and the baby were allowed to stay. Pete spent the night walking around. His eyes are swollen and tired; he looks far older than his 18 years. It was cold last night. He sheltered in doorways, walked round the town several times; was questioned by the police. He eventually took shelter in a derelict house. He is told that there is no chance that he will be re-housed on his own. They go to the VDU. They are second on the list for the area in which they want to be re-housed. It won't be long before it comes up. 'Is there nobody else you could stay with for a week or two?' 'My dad's got a bungalow, but I can't remember where it is. I haven't seen him for two years. I could find it. I could ask my mum, but I don't know where she's living at the moment.'

A man in his forties; greying hair, knitted grey sweater with collar outside a navy blue jacket. He has been living in a furnished room for the past eight years and at last has been given a small council-flat. But the DHSS has refused to make any grant towards furnishing the new place. At the moment, it is empty, with the result that he is still living in the furnished room. He has nothing, is on social security. He has no relatives and is quite alone. 'I haven't got a living soul belonging to me.' 'How's that?' 'Dead. Went away. I don't know.' He feels that DHSS is punishing him for daring to exercise choice in moving from a furnished to an unfurnished place. 'They said, what was wrong with where I was living.' He says he always thought that being able to choose was what made us different from communist countries. 'You know what my trouble is?' 'What?' 'I'm the wrong fucking colour.' 'Why do you say that?' 'It's obvious. Look at who gets preference.' He looks at the interviewer inviting him to collude. He gets no support, so lets it go. A rather fragile official morality keeps some of the wilder expressions of racism in check. He says he must be the only person in Walsall with two flats. 'Not many people who can say that.' 'It's bloody miracle, most people haven't even got one. What else can you do, walk on water?' 'No, but I've skated on some pretty thin ice in my time.'

A lively young woman in her thirties, disabled. She walks with two sticks. Small oval face, bright-blue eyes, wide smile. She left her husband and was offered a home with some friends. 'At least, I thought they were. I agreed to help a bit with the kids to pay for being allowed to stay with them. But they've both gone back to work now, so I'm left being a full-time childminder. One of the kids is three, the other 15 months. It's hard work. Unpaid. If I wanted to look after kids full-time, I'd have my own. I must get out.' The VDU shows where she stands on the waiting list: second in one area, third in another. She lingers in the office, exchanges friendly insults. Many people come in for the sake of the informality and warmth. In some people's lives you can feel the social gap it fills – the sort of conversations occur that might have been associated with the casual exchanges over the garden wall, on the front doorstep; so much casual and informal contact that has been silenced by TV, drowned out by amplified music in public places, stifled by Walkman earpieces, submerged by the clamour of capitalist selling.

A man of 46. He has had cancer for two and a half years and is about to undergo another course of radium treatment that will leave him feeling wretchedly ill. He and his wife want a transfer from the house that is too big for them now that the children are married and live away from home. He has medical priority for transfer and wonders why he has been kept waiting for so long. When the records are checked, it turns out that the medical priority has been wrongly registered in his son's name. His son is married and has moved out. If he had not continued to pester the

Neighbourhood Office, the mistake could have gone on undetected. If it had all been left to the town hall, under the old system, he would never have found out at all. 'It's a bloody horrible place. A woman down the road has bought hers. She's only just finding out what it's going to cost her to put it right. I went to redecorate the bathroom. The scraper went straight through the wood. It's all black with mould. All the skirting board is rotten . . . And they put up new fencing round the garden. All been nicked. I know where it's gone. I know who's had it, and whose pigeon pen it was turned into.' The Neighbourhood Officer says, 'The damp is the same in all those houses.' 'Why can't you get a private firm to do it, a damp injection? They say it's guaranteed a thousand years.' 'Couldn't do that. That'd be privatization. The union wouldn't wear it.' 'The bloody union don't have to live there.'

A young man, perhaps in his late twenties. His frustration has been building up visibly while he has been waiting; shifting from one foot to the other, making noises of impatience. The fencing in his garden has been replaced because it was rotten. Now it has all been ripped up and stolen. The supporting posts weren't driven down deep enough. He has been into the office several times, asking for it to be replaced. As it was done only a few months ago, it isn't going to be given priority. Steve, the assistant, who doesn't always believe in sheltering people from the realities of their situation, says, 'Why don't you put your own fencing up?' 'Because it's not my house.' 'No, but you live there.' 'I rent it from you. It belongs to you.' 'Yes, but I don't have to live there.' 'The kids keep ripping it up.' 'Put your own there, and do it so they can't rip it up.' 'It's not my house.' 'No, but you live there.' 'It's your job.' 'Well, we have to do things in order of how urgent they are. Fencing isn't urgent.' 'Fuck you,' he says, 'it's like talking to a brick wall.' As he goes out, he says, 'Fucking Neighbourhood Offices. I'd put a bomb under 'em.'

A woman of 27, handsome face, fair hair, check coat. Her five-year son has muscular dystrophy. She has come for advice; to find out what adaptations are possible for the house, if she decides to keep him at home. 'There are several kinds of dystrophy, they've told us. The one he's got is the worst there is. They didn't know for a long time what was wrong with him. It was the worst time, the not knowing. We've been everywhere with him, I've been in the hospital with him in Birmingham, then Oxford. They've told us now that there isn't any hope that he'll get better. All we can expect is a slow deterioration. We're living with my father and I've been looking after him since mother died. I don't know what to do for the best. We have to decide – do we send him away to school, where he would be with other children, and with people who are trained to look after him, or do we keep him with us? The trouble is, however well qualified people are, there's nobody will give him the love we can, and part of you thinks that's what he needs above everything. You want to do what's best for him, only you don't know what the best is. Who is the best judge, the parents or the doctors?' She says that if there were more support in the neighbourhood, she would not hesitate to keep him at home. But the unrelieved intensity and anxiety of looking after a dying child is frightening. She has one sister; but she has her own problems. You can't expect anything of neighbours these days – 'Oh, they're very good, they'll do anything for you, as long as they don't get involved. "If there's anything we can do," they say, "let us know." But that isn't what it means. It means anything but commitment, and that's the one thing you need.'

There seem to be so many of these convoluted relationships, the changing constellations of individuals make a mockery of all the official ideas of what constitutes a family. But unhappily, for the poorest, it isn't a liberation from a constricting straitjacket: in the swirling confusion, the maelstrom of passions and resentment, the shifting affections and withdrawn commitment, the children learn, above all else, the unpredictability of those who care for them, the unreliability of adults. You sense the actual manufacture of a great deal of deferred unhappiness, the uncertain identity, the broken continuity, a cynicism in children, an ugly premature knowledge that you have to look after yourself and that to survive you have to be hard.

The next day at Blakenall, the office had stopped taking repairs. The union was in dispute with council. The backlog of unfinished repairs was already increasing, because of the accumulated unmet need over the years of neglect. One of the problems is that in some areas the workers of the direct labour force don't have the same concern for the success of the Neighbourhood Offices as those who set them up and staff them. The employer remains the employer. This means that there are frequent overlaps, failures to co-ordinate certain jobs, work wrongly reported. There are frequent complaints about a pile of sand that has been standing so long it's been washed away by the rain, that bricks or wood have been nicked, fencing broken, urgent repairs on door or window-catches not carried out, so that people are afraid to go out for fear of break-ins. ('They're watching. I know who they are,' one woman cried, almost in tears; 'the minute you go out that door, they'll be in there like a load of monkeys, picking over your bits and pieces.')

To tell the people that no further repairs were being accepted was received by most of them with incomprehension. 'What do you mean, accepted?' one man asked, 'I'm telling you the fucking window's broken. It isn't a matter of accepting it. It's bust.' Dispute? What dispute? It all felt disturbingly familiar; a bit like the old system which the Neighbourhood Offices are supposed to have done away with; there is the familiar shrug of resignation, the what-can-you-expect? weariness. It was as though you could feel the goodwill generated by the neighbourhood scheme evaporate far more swiftly than it had been built up.

A woman in her late thirties. She looks me in the eye. 'You don't talk Blakenall, you're not from here. What do you want to come here for? Worse place in the world, this is. Why? They'd take the bread off your plate here. You used to be able to leave your door open day and night. Not any more.' The two children with her are crying for sweets. She smacks them both, then gives them a tube of Smarties. 'Do you want to adopt one? You can have them both for a fiver. Some days I think they'll drive me mad. Second marriage. I should have learnt one was enough. I haven't seen him for six months. There's women all over Wolverhampton got his kids. Maintenance? It's like trying to get blood out of a stone. And he's a stone all right. Hard and cold.' But she says it cheerfully enough; and when she has spoken, she accepts a cigarette and seems ready to settle in for a chat. Only there are so many people waiting.

An elderly couple, woman in her seventies, man in his late sixties. He wears a raincoat, neat moustache; she is wearing a straw hat and navy-blue gloves and smart shoes. Both have been widowed and have recently married. They want a transfer from her house, where they have been living. The affection between them irradiates the whole room. 'You look well on it.' 'I went to the doctor with me chest. He says, "Get a divorce, that'll put you right." ' They exude a rare gaiety, and everybody else's conversation stops. 'We want a smaller place than we've got now.' 'How about a bungalow by the sea?' 'I don't care where we go as long as it's not down Drake Road.' 'Why, what's wrong with Drake Road?' 'What's wrong with it? They only put them there to kick the bucket. They do. I know umpteen that's happened to. Sommat in the water. I don't mind where else you put us. Only it's took me all me life to find him and I don't want to lose him yet awhile.'

One of the less tangible advantages of the Neighbourhood Offices is that even though people often don't understand the system, at least they *feel* that these are places where you can talk freely. A woman in her mid-fifties, dressed in her best, obviously very proud. She starts hesitantly. She isn't one to tell everybody her business. Three years ago her husband died and she took in a lodger, an elderly man who had nowhere to go, 'I met him in the pub. He seemed all right, he reminded me of my own father. We had a joint tenancy on the house. I wouldn't marry him, but he was company and we suited each other. He said he was a widower; anyway, he's gone. He just cleared off one day. Somewhere in Wales, he didn't say where he was going. He went out one night and never came back. It's a big place, Wales. I can't go and look for him. Anyway, the Social won't pay the rent direct while he's still on the book and not living there. But he's got to sign it to say he's given up his part of the tenancy. I didn't know what I was doing when I agreed to the joint tenancy. I thought that would put us on the same level, like. I can't go and look for him. And I must have my affairs in order. It just shows what happens when you try to help people. I thought he was genuine. It isn't worth it. I know one thing, I've learnt me lesson, I shan't make the mistake of trying to help anybody else in the future.'

A man who has been out of work for over a year: long ginger sideburns, a shabby grey suit, worn-out shoes, bitten fingernails. His wife has left him; he says, 'It was only the money I was earning that kept us together.' He had been a scaffolder. He has over £1,000 worth of arrears. Faced with the hopelessness of paying it off, he has become depressed. A pound a week. Fifty pounds a year. 'That means I'll have a clear rent book in 20 years' time, providing I don't fall behind again. I'd sooner do a life sentence.' Tattooed on his fingers TRUE LOVE. He has tried to erase the tattoo himself, but the marks remain – all he has done is to make his fingers red and sore. He says he tried to rub it off with a wire brush. 'Fucking cow. She's walked out on me. A man can't look after three kids on his own.' And his house expresses the demoralization and sadness of a man unaccustomed to looking after children; the debris of sketchy meals – packets of bread, packets of butter, piles of dirty plates; washing everywhere, dust on the furniture. He says, 'I'm the only bloke in Walsall who'd have to win the pools to pay off his rent.'

A tough-looking man in his early thirties; short hair, pugnacious, proud of his muscular body. He says he was in the army in Cyprus when he was 18; he has seen people killed; his mate was blown up, his body broken. He used not to be afraid of anything. For the past three years he has been suffering from agoraphobia; and people in the community, in the family, don't understand. 'I was with my father one dinner-time, playing snooker up the club, and he died the same evening. Just like that. That's when my trouble started. My father was a mate. We used to do everything together. We used to go up the club, betting-shop, we shared the pigeons. We were always together. People think I'm just swinging it. I can't go out without Kath; we're not married, but we've been living together for a couple of years. We've two children – two, and a month old. Kath understands. Without her, I don't know what I'd do. People think you're funny. My brother doesn't understand. They tell me there's only one person who can cure it and that's myself. It'll come on suddenly. Being on the road does it, a gap in a wall, a hole between two buildings, an open space . . . I can't do it on my own. Coming down here this morning, it was purgatory, I close my eyes and hang on to her. It can hit you any minute. I feel I'm not in control. People don't believe a man can feel like that. They say "Pull yourself together." I can't. I never used to have any patience with people who had problems like that. But I understand now.'

There is never enough time to follow through all the things that people bring into the office, even when, as in this man's case, the cause of the illness isn't far to seek. He recognizes it himself when he connects the onset of his fears with the suddeness of his father's death. And yet, so many painful experiences go unrecognized; and they fester and get worse, as the isolated individual tries to deal with them as his private hurt. There are social wounds, there are areas of suffering which we scarcely acknowledge; things that require a more imaginative and understanding community. It isn't difficult to see ways in which the extension of the neighbourhood idea could act as a healing and confidence-creating influence. The need is there; only it easily gets submerged by what look like more urgent practical concerns.

A man, shabby, fat, unshaven, in a shapeless gabardine raincoat. He wears a threadbare shirt with grimy collar and cuffs. He sits slumped on the plastic chair in front of the desk, hands loosely clasped; a picture of defeat, shoulders rounded. He used to be a labourer for the council, but he finished 18 months ago. He has arthritis of the spine and was found at the same time to have a shadow on his lung. He has been in court for arrears that came to more than £1,100. He lives alone in the council house where he was brought up and where his mother and father died. He has short curly hair, once black, not grey exactly, but faded; his expression is one of complete passivity and indifference. He wants a transfer from the house; since he has been disabled, he finds the stairs impossible to manage; half the house is wasted with disuse. 'Shall I put you down for the Beechdale Estate?' 'If you like.' The tone is one of absolute compliance. He cannot fill in the form because he has never learned to read. His sister comes to see him once a week and reads any letters to him. He says, 'I don't suppose I shall ever work again. I'm finished. I reckon that's about it.' The shadow on his lung has cleared; the arthritis prevents him from doing any heavy work, it's true; but there is something so dispirited about him. 'I'm finished,' he says again. 'How old are you?' He says, 'Thirty-two.' The posture of being finished, on the scrap heap, done for, has a tragic finality about it; and there are some people who embrace it almost gratefully; but there is something deeply shocking when people who are still young find relief in this attitude. There are those even younger than this man who fall into it – I think of the boy of 19 who proudly boasted that he could sleep 17 or 18 hours a day if he tried; a kind of competitiveness in defeat. He said, 'I'm an expert at sleep'; and found comfort in the ability to distinguish himself, even in something so negative as his effaced consciousness; a metaphor somehow for so many of the redundant and unwanted energies of young people in the current phase of capitalism.

In contrast, some of those older people shaped by a more coercive and cruel discipline haven't wasted away, but have maintained their self-respect. A man of 60 who was made redundant a year ago is suffering real hardship. His wife lost her job at the same time. He has devoted the last 12 months to his allotment, growing vegetables and flowers, a couple of fruit trees. It helps out, not only with their own food, but he also gives away the surplus produce. 'I always try to take something to the pub Sunday dinner-time. Not to sell. I don't believe in selling. I worked in a foundry for 43 years, same place. The foundry was hot, dirty and dangerous when I started at 14 and it stayed hot, dirty and dangerous until it closed, a year ago ... That's why I always loved the pigeons and the allotment. The sky and the earth, they're two things about as far away from the foundry as you can get. A man who loves pigeons, his wife might not see for days on end, but she'll know he's not off after some other woman. I always used to come out of the foundry and straight to the allotment, the part of the year it was light. I could see the fruits of my labour there, in a way that I couldn't at work. I felt I'd achieved something. I grew everything – potatoes, beans, carrots, peas, onions, beetroot, apples and plums. I'm a foundryman through and through. I've always been a Labour man. I'll never change, whatever they try to tell us.' He has come to the office because now that his unemployment benefit has run out, his social security claim hasn't come through. He and his wife have been living for the past month on £26 a week.

A young couple, poorly dressed, thin, she with dull fair hair, he with long dark sideburns and a cross in his ear. They place a damp-stained blue sheet and white cloth, discoloured by mildew, on the desk with the care that you might take of exhibits in a courtroom. 'What's this?' These are some of the things from the bedroom where they are sleeping with a four-month old baby. Nothing stays dry. 'The Health Officer told us to bring them down.' The houses are due to be modernized and treatment of condensation is one of the things to be tackled. When? 'I can't say exactly when. The money has run out.' 'The money hasn't run out for the blacks and the scroungers, or the prostitutes and drug addicts, has it?'

One of the most glaring things about the burden of anxiety and unhappiness that people bring to the Neighbourhood Offices is the way in which they see their own problems, not as socially produced, but as a personal visitation. They reflect the dominant ideology, the ideology of the rich and successful, who insist that the rewards they reap are directly due to their worth and moral stature. It follows, therefore, that the poor are where they are because of their lack of merit. And there is so little resistance to that falsehood in these poor places. So many of the people who can buy their way out of the poor estates have gone. It is significant that few of the council houses in Blakenall have been sold to the sitting tenants. In this way, the poorest areas cease to be real communities, because people know that they are not there from choice. If the poor come to prey on each other, the rich and powerful can point to their despair and say, 'Look, they are where they are because that is what they deserve.' The deterrence of poverty is a greater spur than the impulse to gain wealth: many people who aren't particularly grasping or ruthless or money-grabbing find themselves nevertheless caught in an endless treadmill, the rat-race, as it's sometimes described, not because of their desire for riches, but because the alternative of slipping back into poverty is such a cruel threat.

This does not mean that the majority of people in Blakenall in their personal dealings are not kind, helpful and neighbourly. It isn't that. It isn't that people won't do the shopping for the housebound and infirm, it isn't that the unemployed youngsters won't help dig someone's garden, that neighbours won't keep an eye on the vulnerable, look after each other's kids; indeed, there are always examples of charity collections for children who are handicapped and for those who need to receive specialist medical care that can't be had on the NHS. But it is a disengagement from each other at a deeper level: the not getting involved, keeping your head down, staying out of trouble, closing your front door, walking by on the other side.

It is impossible to escape the irony that on this estate at half past seven on Monday and Wednesday evenings a very considerable number of the people are watching Coronation Street on TV: that frozen, eternal working-class street, where fictitious lives have come to take on such significance for us. Do they offer us a sense of continuity when there seems to be so little in real life? Does the shadow of community give us reassurance of a substance that has departed? There is something more than soap opera for the millions of people who watch it each week: it has the fascination of something that endures, when the actual communities it claims to represent are in the throes of dissolution and change. There is, in so many areas of our lives, a sense of helpless spectatorship. Things happen without our consent, beyond our control. The definition of politics has become more and more narrow, as increasingly important areas of our lives are declared to be beyond the reach of politics, out of bounds; with the result that the only political question in the mainstream comes to be 'How are we to make the economy grow?' Once the logic of this reductive view is accepted, we find ourselves accepting everything that follows, all the contradictions and absurdities. For instance, we are now being told that we can no longer afford many of the services that have come to be associated with the welfare state, we must cut them, because we are too poor to sustain them. But when the welfare state was established in the 1940s, we had just lived through a devastating war. We were in a state of great austerity and impoverishment and yet it was still possible to fund the health service, to create the first ever comprehensive welfare provision for all the people. Now, 35 years later, we have to cut these services. Is this because we are poorer now than we were then? Is it because need has increased? How can this be, given the spectacular rise in wealth over the past 35 years? Which parts of the argument are being suppressed and for whose benefit? How is it possible that the kind of suffering to be found on any poor estate, in any city centre area, in any ghetto or poor district, seems to be beyond remedy? The disaffection and cynicism of people are a direct result of the diminishing of the area of political debate, the exclusion of issues that are of vital importance to us. The logic of the system has invaded our lives so deeply that we have come to accept the unacceptable, to tolerate the intolerable, to defend the morally indefensible. In other words, we have accepted the subordination of human needs to the needs and demands of capital as if it really were a law of nature.

The Neighbourhood Offices, by going back into the places where people live, suggest all kinds of questions that have been outlawed in the political debate that no longer envisages any possibility outside the workings of capitalism. For instance, they pose questions about the nature of community and solidarity. What can we do together and for each other? Is it thinkable that we might consider deprofessionalizing some of the expertise that hasn't brought us any great measure of happiness – social work and education for a start. Is it possible that we could dare to believe in each other, that we could offer each other our company and our time more generously; that we might be able to create solace and comfort as well as the diversion and amusement that has been appropriated by the entertainment industries; that we might start to talk to each other, even to dare to exchange ideas, in place of the pre-packaged and carefully pruned substitutes for them that come to us from the media; that we have skills and energies that could be applied to the material and psychological well-being of one another. These should be only some of the implications of a world in which we dared to take control of our own lives. People, we might even discover, become the richest resource of all; the whole immobile and unshakeable structures of society start to look less powerful once you start to ask whom they serve and who makes the sacrifice to keep them in place. We might even glimpse the great lie at the heart of it all – that money is the cement holding together a system that is there to serve money.

As long as Neighbourhood Offices can be seen as simply a mechanism for devolving limited services, they remain unthreatening, unlikely to radicalize people. But with the imagination and creative understanding of those who first conceived them, their growth and extension, their thrust into the heart of the alien ideology in whose shadow we all live, becomes a real living possibility.

3. Goscote: the renewal of neighbourhood

I think the worst thing I've seen in a Neighbourhood Office was an officer debt-counselling a woman who had big rent arrears. This woman had bought two bags of chips and the counsellor wrote down in the book that these chips cost her 40 pence and this woman's children hadn't eaten all the chips. So the debt counsellor said, 'If you'd all had a little less each, you could have saved 20 pence there.' This counsellor has got a job at £9,000 a year.

— Trainee housing assistant

Goscote is an estate that has been spectacularly improved since the coming of the Neighbourhood Offices. The very name of Goscote was once sufficient to deny people credit in shops all over Walsall. If you told people your address, you were looked at askance and strangers wondered what was the matter with you that you should have 'finished up' there – as though Goscote was a final destination.

It is a small estate, something over 400 houses, built in the 1930s. But from being a place apart, an estate of outcasts, it has become much sought after. Indeed, it has been transformed. Much of the credit for this must go to the neighbourhood officer, who came here from Liverpool, and whose energy and enthusiasm have done so much. As Ken Thompson himself admits, it shouldn't depend upon the commitment of individuals. The ambition of the neighbourhood idea must be to leave in place organizations of the people themselves, who will assure continuity and maintenance of services; who will themselves be vigilant and control the running of their communities.

Goscote is surrounded by water: an area that floods readily after any significant rain to the south, the canal to the west, the sewage farm to the east. Many poorer estates were built on ill-drained land, were placed out of the way, were provided with amenities that were second-rate and have been decaying ever since – often in a far less dramatic way than some of the tower blocks and slum estates of more recent years but with a longer history of fatalism and neglect. It is far from easy to mobilize the people who live here.

When Ken Thompson was first appointed, and came to Goscote in November 1981, he made a point of talking to every person who lived on the estate. There were then 280 families. One hundred and thirty-two houses stood empty – 'voids' as they are picturesquely called in local authority terminology. The reputation for being hard to let was justified: 121 houses and 11 bungalows were unoccupied. Eighteen months later, every house is allocated and there is a waiting list for the area. Goscote really was a slough of despond, a place of internal exile to which the poorest people were directed; it is tempting to say transported. You can still see the signs of what it was like is some parts of the estate. By the early 1980s, vandalism – not merely in the pursuit of theft, but as wanton large-scale destruction – was making house after house uninhabitable. If a tenant gave notice that he or she was moving, neighbours would help load the van or waggon and, the moment they had gone, the house would be invaded by people, ripping out copper tubing, kitchen units, lavatories, bathroom fittings, every-thing detachable. There was a brisk trade in copies of front-door keys; sometimes an impression of the same key was sold to several people; and then arguments occurred about who had first claim on the pickings. The first week Ken Thompson was here, he saw two women in the street fighting over a radiator that had been taken from an empty property. 'If her's got one, I want one.' 'But you've got a coal fire.' 'I don't care, I want it.' (The story of people stealing things for the sake of possession is quite common;

possession itself seems desirable, regardless either of use or even of potential for re-sale.)

Ken collected a great deal of information about the estate. Sixty per cent of the occupants were pensioners; illiteracy or semi-literacy was over 50 per cent. There was a higher incidence of all social evils than in any other local estate; and that in spite of the predominance of elderly people. There were more births to girls of 15 and 14, wife and child abuse, children in care, prostitution. Many of the people who had come here were originally tinkers, tatters, unemployed, under-employed; they brought with them the habits of eking out an existence on the margins of the economy – carts, horses, barrows, donkeys, stalls. There was even a case where an internal wall had been torn down to accommodate a horse in one of the houses. Goscote never recovered from its original purpose and remained a dumping ground for 40 years.

Ken: 'It was built on marshy land. People used to talk of the Goscote smell. It was thought to be the sewage farm. But sewage farms don't smell. They shouldn't, anyway. But everybody accepted it, it was part of the folklore. And it was true – the kids were always sniffling and had sore throats. When I asked why, the mothers said, "Oh, it's always like that." There was this deep sense of resignation.

'I guessed that there was something wrong that could be remedied if the will to do it was there. There were a lot of blocked drains. It took 15 months to convince the bureaucracy. All the sewage from Blakenall and Cosford was coming across a field that was constantly being flooded. There were plagues of rats from time to time. These rats were mostly concentrated in the south-east corner of the estate; and in a lot of the toilets in that part the sewage was all coming back up after you pulled the chain. Nobody was inclined to do anything about it. They didn't believe me. It had got so bad in some of the houses that people were going to the lavatory in a bucket and going to dump it over the fields – the toilets were unusable. Eventually, it turned out that one of the main egress points of the sewers was blocked by some links from a huge anchor chain – obviously something dumped years ago; it had broken the sewer and blocked it. So it means that none of the sewage was getting from Goscote to the sewage farm; it had all collected in the pipes. And then the drains had been crushed in many places – nine-inch, 18-inch pipes had been smashed by gipsy waggons or horses or whatever in some of the gardens. We finally located sewer collapses all over the place. It meant that the whole estate was on a bed of sewage and God knows how long it had been like that; it had been escaping for years. One hundred and twenty-five thousand pounds was allocated to sort it out. I inspected the whole system and had all the manhole covers replaced by the heavy blind covers. What had been happening was that as soon as the manhole covers were placed, they were being taken up and sold by tatters, so a lot of them had been covered up by bits of wood or sacking. They were very dangerous.

'Of course a lot of people didn't like what I was doing. And I don't mean just the bureaucracy. I was moving in on some people's livelihood on the estate – those who had been ripping off public property for years. They didn't like it. One day, two blokes drove at me in a car, it swerved right on to the green where I was walking. I jumped on to a garden wall, otherwise they would have had me.

'One day I was walking through the estate and I saw some kids throwing bricks at a rat in a back garden. I went in and kicked the rat, stamped on it. Next thing that happened, his mother reported me to the RSPCA. For a rat. She said, "What do you mean by killing animals in front of kids?" Some people have no idea. Same week, I came across an old-age pensioner and he told me he'd got a rat in his living-room. He said, "Come and see if you can catch the bugger." I went in and there, in the middle of the carpet, sat this bloody great rat, cleaning its whiskers and watching the television. I said, "I'll send for the rat-catcher." I went outside and we'd got some Task Force youngsters working on the estate; and one of these lads was going by and he just happened to have a ferret up his jumper. I said, "Lend us your ferret a minute." So we put it in this room and it went for the rat, had it in a minute. Next day, I'm walking down the street and there's three pensioners talking on the corner. One of them says, "Is that right you breed ferrets in your office to catch the rats?" You feel you must be on fairly strong ground, plague of rats, danger of epidemics. At times, I felt it was like the Middle Ages, you know, the Black Death was going to be the next thing. But I underestimated the bureaucracy. I rang the environmental health department. "There's rats in Goscote. Could you give us some advice?" "Oh, you speak to public works." So I ring public works. "Where are the rats?" "Goscote." "No, are they above ground or below ground? If they're below ground, they're our responsibility, if they're above, you'll have to ring the environmental health department." "You're kidding me." "No," they said, "that's the way it works." I said, "Whose responsibility is it if they're in the bloody roof – the RAF?" It turned out that if they were actually in your house, the environmental health were in charge.'

The feeling that he was disturbing settled attitudes and habits accompanied everything Ken did. The conservatism of the poor goes deep: it isn't fecklessness or apathy, as is sometimes claimed, but the only sensible response to a situation they have always known and which never changes. In addition, many of the more enterprising tenants had been carrying on unofficial businesses – scrap metal, wood, spare parts, stray consignments and lorryloads of all kinds. It took many months to dig up some of the gardens, to exacavate the decaying debris and rubbish that had accumulated, rotted away, sunk into the marshy earth beneath. Some of the garden levels were almost as high as the bay windows. A few of these excavations were still going on: they involved earth removers digging sometimes to a depth of several feet: ancient wheels, bicycle frames, posts, poles, decayed and rusty machinery, the remains of pigeon pens and hen-runs, lumps of concrete, demolished outhouses, rotten wood, rabbit hutches, broken handcarts, boxes, tins, all tightly compressed and overgrown with weeds, grass and brambles. Trees had taken root, a growth of hawthorn, wild roses, buddleia.

Ken: 'When I first started, there were about three people active in the tenants' association. They had fought for Goscote, in spite of everything. There was just the handful of people who'd kept alive the hope that something would be done for the place eventually. There had been plans issued by the council for the re-furbishing of Goscote, after one of those patronizing public-relations consultations, which hardly anybody responds to. You know the kind of thing, exhibition in the town hall, little models, alternative plans A, B, and C. None of them bore any relation to the needs or aspirations of the residents. They were all drawn up by professionals, all those who know best, whose job it is to know what we want. Plan A was to demolish the whole estate. Plan B was to demolish 97 houses on the outer edge of the estate, leaving just the central core. Plan C was to demolish between 38 and 48 houses. Significantly, they all involved the destruction of houses. Plan C was the one that had been chosen before I arrived. I threw it in the bin. I said, "We're not going to have housing stock torn down, when there is such a crying need, and so little is being built." It was in the middle of the first Thatcher government, the housing budget had borne the brunt of all the public spending cuts. The Labour council was more sympathetic, and they said, "Right, you've got £400,000 to spend. Go ahead."

'I worked seven days a week. A hundred hours sometimes. I'm not kidding, you had to work at speed, if you weren't going to be overwhelmed by the sheer amount of inertia and decay of the place. If you weren't careful, you'd clear a bit here and then, as soon as you turned your back, it'd all get spoilt again. I think that's the secret of any new administration coming in, of any new appointment. There's no substitution for getting on with it. People make the mistake of spending too much time feeling their way around, getting briefed: that means being prejudiced by all those who don't want anything new to happen, being told a thousand reasons why nothing can be done.

'I was allocating houses at quarter to twelve at night sometimes, getting people in before they were gutted or ripped apart. I was told afterwards that the longest anybody expected me to stay here was three months. For the first few weeks I just made my presence felt, talked to everybody. This was a no-go area for the rent-collectors then. They had so much aggravation, there had been so many assaults, they actually gave up collecting the rents, except on the outer part of the estate on the main road. They wouldn't go into the interior: like the jungle it was, impenetrable. So they had to rely on people paying their rent at the town hall. But the funny thing was, although there were some big debtors, on the whole Goscote has some of the cleanest rent books in Walsall. When I first went round and saw some of the conditions, those who'd got bad debts would show me round and say, "Would you pay rent for living here?" And you had to admit, you wouldn't.'

The state of some of the houses was appalling at that time. There are still a few like it now – one old man with half a dozen dogs has an accumulation of dog-shit all over the house and it is almost unbearable inside; but he is very old and won't let anyone into his house. Most of the houses have been improved beyond recognition. There were broken toilets, holes in the roof, gaps in the wall where bricks had been removed, doors had been removed, used as firewood or sold for scrap; some of the houses had virtually no furniture, were verminous; there were soiled mattresses on the floor and old coats for bedclothes. The gardens were often full of garbage, overspilled dustbins, dogs and cats scavenging among the waste. Some of the kitchens were covered with an accumulation of grease and dust that had become embedded it it. When Ken told one woman to clean up her house, she said, 'Why, what's wrong with it?' Ken says, 'If you take away people's dignity by telling them they've no choice but to live in a piggery, they'll conform to it by living like pigs.

'I sent out a newsletter. What I needed to do was get a breakdown of the circumstances of every tenant. That way, I could find out which day their benefit was paid and then I'd aim to get the rent collected the day after. I knew that if you did what the rent man always did traditionally, that is, call every other week on a Friday, you'd get no money. That's the way to build up big arrears, because, by then, there's nothing left. For most people, it's a question of first come, first paid, as long as the money lasts. So I got to know which day the various benefits were paid from DHSS. Of course, they stop it at source now. But I found out invalidity benefit was paid on Monday, war pension and old-age pension on Tuesday and Thursday, dole money Friday and Saturday. So I arranged with the tenants for the rent to be picked up the day after giro arrived. It was very successful.

'The only thing that has harmed us is the lad who was collecting the rents, he's gone a bit haywire. He disappeared with all the records and about £5,000; so far, we've only managed to get back £800. He had got into drugs; he'd had a bad time. That's one of the hazards. He'd entered all the payments into the tenants' rent books accurately, but he never kept the office records up, with the result that we don't know who owes what. If people find out what's happened, there's nothing to stop them altering their rent books and we shall never find out who owes what, whether it's been paid or not. That's one of the risks. It isn't an indictment of the system.

'I made a lot of enemies in the bureaucracy. I sent out a circular, saying that the authority was robbing the public by actually creating rent arrears. It emerged that a lot of those with arrears ought to have been on rent and rates rebate. Some of them said they had applied for a rebate but had heard no more about it. This story came back again and again. So I raised it with the civic centre. "Oh yes, we've probably received the applications, but we're inundated with work." I couldn't believe it. "But this is people's lives, their pitiful income." I took a rebate form to them and said, "Back-date this 18 months." "You what?" "I want this back-dated. She applied 18 months ago." "You can't do things like this. Three weeks is the most we ever give back-dated." So I had this altercation with the rebate department. I found out that the law states that you can back-date 12 months from the date of application if the circumstances warrant it. And I had the temerity to tell this to the bureaucracy. I found out there was a lack of knowledge in the Neighbourhood Offices about the possibility of using rebates back-dated to knock down the arrears. With this system of rebates, we could legitimately wipe out large amounts of arrears. For every £1,000 of rebate over a year, you got £900 of it back from central government. The bureaucracy said, "We shall decide on back-dating."

'They argued about it. It came to council. The chairman of housing got up and said, "Have we been robbing the public, blah blah blah," made a great to-do about it. Nobody knew. It went away to be legally verified. The civic centre hated it. I've always believed in sharing knowledge. I wasn't going to conceal what I considered a wrong that had been done to the people who could least afford it.

They had me down at the civic centre. They couldn't reprimand me, because I was right. They said, "You're a housing manager now, behave like one." It means that you're part of a club, you have to accept the rules.

'I also found out that in certain circumstances, you can back-date longer than 12 months. They said I was wrong. All right, take it to the courts. What they couldn't forgive was that I hadn't gone to them first. It would have looked better if it had come through as official housing policy. But it wasn't housing policy. "We weren't aware . . ." They bloody well should have been aware. The thing that bureaucracy hates more than anything else is being made fools of.

'So all the people who said they had filled in rebate forms, we took it as understood, we assumed it had got lost somewhere in the maw of bureaucracy. We took it that every tenant who was entitled to rebate had applied for it and it had got lost. We were using the system correctly. And we wiped off a load of arrears.

'I think people accept that you're trying to do something for them. They know when you're bullshitting and when you're not. But the other side of it is that you can then ask them to play fair with you. We had to re-educate a number of people into paying rent. It was a process of education. You had to extort the money sometimes. But it worked. It was a bloody success. Everything had gone to pieces, arrears rocketed, people hadn't renewed rebates because they didn't know they had to, their rents had gone up and they just couldn't pay.

'The next thing was to give people what they most needed for the houses. First thing, new roofs. Guttering, windowframes; then the complete modernization programme. Boundary walls, that was another thing – a lot of them had been knocked down or just fallen into a heap of stones. We built up all the front walls, they're rough grey-brick walls with a regular coping on top. That gave people a sense of limits, the boundaries that had disappeared; dogs, kids, people used to take short cuts, almost as if people's gardens didn't exist. That's what encouraged people to use all public space as a tip; just throw things down, it didn't matter because it didn't belong to anybody.

'The secret is actually to make the system work as it should operate in theory, but was never meant to in practice. If somebody was moving, we'd clear up the property, get it ready by 4 p.m., not wait for the DHSS grant to come through before the next people moved in but get them in right away. Ring up waste disposal, get the Direct Labour Office (DLO) to clear the garden, or whatever. Then we'd get a load of the new tenant's furniture, stick it in the house. We had a good relationship with the DLO, they got a full time-sheet, the tenant was satisfied, the council was satisfied. Working the system became a full-time occupation. We couldn't have done it without the lads from the DLO. Two blokes were assigned to me full-time; and there was a basis of trust between us.

'After May 1982, the Labour Party asked me to step back a bit, stay in the background. They felt they were vulnerable to attacks on the neighbourhood scheme and I'd stirred things up a bit. I did it, but everything started to go downhill. It proves that you can't get things done without a lot of individual energy and commitment. It's not good relying on the workings of the system. You've got to have somebody who is going to give the time and the energy and the strength of involvement to it.

'In November 1981, when I came here, there were 145 crimes a month being committed in Goscote – that's out of only 350 occupied houses. That's about 1,800 crimes a year – about four to a house. Everything was being ripped off. There had been a modernization programme initiated in 1975 but it had been only partially completed – 30 per cent, I believe. The money had run out because of theft and vandalism. It was obvious that some security was needed. That was one of the first things I saw to. It costs £334 a week to provide security on the estate, including weekends. I had to fight to get it. It sounds like a lot of money, but the logic of how much it saves speaks for itself. You can't exactly estimate it, but it must be thousands a week. The office opened in January 1982. By September of that year, crimes were averaging two a month. In 1981, there had been 86 crimes of damage to property. These have decreased dramatically.'

Those who work on repairs confirm this spectacular drop in damage to the houses. It has made their work more interesting and satisfying. They say that previously they didn't really have any incentive to care about whether they worked well or badly, because the odds were that every job they did would be ruined within a few days. But now they can see the effect of their labour which, after all, has been the single biggest contribution to the transformation of the estate. The workers have their own stories and folklore about the jobs they have been called to: the thieves who demolished the whole side wall of a house because when they went to get the bath downstairs it got stuck; the house where the horse was stabled in the stairwell; the house that had been used as an aviary and was covered with years of bird-droppings.

Ken worked out a comprehensive programme of repairs with the Direct Labour Office. But there remained the problem of vandalism. 'I got sick of going before a Magistrates' Court, and then the council picking up the tab. So I had a word with the copper here. There was one guy, he was a right villain. He had committed the worst vandalism and destruction on a house that I'd ever seen. I said to the copper, "Why don't you do him for criminal damage? That's a Crown Court job." I went into the property, and listed every item of damage, theft, wrecking. I costed it in every detail – working-hours required for the repair, every item missing, the lot. It came to £9,000 worth of damage and £912 worth of theft. I went to the council's legal department. I said I was going to do it as the neighbourhood officer. It came to court and he got 18 months' jail. The judge gave us damages of £9,000. Insurance companies only pay up if there's a conviction, otherwise the local authority has to carry the cost. It's like the electricity meters. If there's no conviction, the tenant gets debited for the amount missing. We ran a poster campaign and we used the pictures of the damage this man had done.'

Ken was moved out of Goscote at the end of 1982. He had been too vigorous in his disturbance of the official structures. It was felt that his conspicuous work might antagonize the anti-Labour coalition that had replaced the Labour council. He was moved to the Blakenall office. The people of Goscote drew up a petition to have him reinstated. He told them to drop it. 'I'd got really choked off, slogging your tripes out, and then getting treated like shit.' But the residents drew up a second petition. Everybody on the estate signed, with only two refusals. Ken was amazed: he had spent much of his time acting tough, telling people off, chivvying and upbraiding them. He has no sentimentality about the place. 'You can't close your eyes to the endless ripping off; it's the poor preying on those who are even poorer. There's nothing glamorous or radical about working-class crime. It just turns the neighbourhood into a sort of private enterprise law and order – a caricature of the values of the official morality of society; and the strong intimidate the weak, and the better off get the hell out of it as quickly as they can.

'I suppose the council didn't like the way I'd challenged the bureaucracy, the authority. I went to Blakenall and was there 11 weeks. In Goscote, while I was away, everything fell apart. Crime went up by 370 per cent; applications for properties here ceased, the number of people wanting to get out rocketed again. It made me feel good, but bloody sorry; not only for the worker who'd been in here, but because of the fact that one individual could make that much difference. It's the opposite of the way things should be. I was providing a focus and centre for the community and that's wrong. What I've been working towards since then is the aim of leaving in place a structure that won't depend on one single person. In the end, it is the people who have to make the decisions and then it won't matter who is here.

'When I first arrived, Goscote Community Association consisted of just a few people who were making a fantastic effort, but they had no real power behind them – behind them was the fatalism and acceptance of all the things that are wrong about the place. You need to have a mass following, so that anything you say will be listened to. Even so, Mrs Smith has done a great job. What has happened has been that the Tenants' Association now has a positive say in who comes to live here. That's not to say they have an arbitrary veto. But people round here, they know each other's families, and if somebody is known to be violent or has got a bad record, they can say no. The only thing you can't allow is racism. You can't discriminate against people on the grounds of colour. But if a place has been a rubbish dump for years, you've got to turn round a certain percentage of the people, leaven it a bit. That's the only way you'll create a different feeling, give the area a bit of self-respect. You can only do that by weeding out some of the real villains.'

Of course, this does mean that the villains are simply moved on elsewhere; but certainly if there is some dispersal, there is at least a chance that one single neighbourhood won't become burdened with too many of them. The concentration of the poorest and the least able in one place does not create a sort of anarchic and radical alternative to capitalism, as some left-inclined romantics imagine. It actually makes for an atmosphere of terror, a network of intimidation; the kind of ghetto that is an incipient version of the poorest inner-city areas of the United States. The consequences of that should comfort no one: the poor simply eat each other up; and they can be relied upon to do so by the rich and powerful, who can then point to the way they live and say that they are where they are because that is all they deserve.

After the second petition, Ken returned to Goscote. The office itself is simply a couple of houses that have been converted, right at the heart of the estate. In that sense, it isn't at all typical of the Neighbourhood Offices. But because it serves a smaller area than Blakenall, there are never long queues. Ken knows everyone, there is a fairly casual coming and going. People linger for a talk. They can be themselves and don't have to assume that curiously stilted behaviour that working-class people have always felt was proper with officials – a sort of virtuous piety that is intended to placate those with power. If you feel like swearing you can swear, and the expression of feeling is not prohibited. It is a relaxed place; and that doesn't happen automatically but is a response to the feeling that goes out from it.

'When I first came to Goscote, I had to have a showdown with the guy who everybody knew was the cock of Goscote. The head of the local mafia, a great brick shithouse of a bloke, big man – his main source of income was vandalizing council properties. He'd go and strip them and leave two Alsatians on guard outside to stop any of the lesser villains from muscling in. I calculated, on a conservative estimate, that in his time he must have caused around half a million quids' worth of damage. One night, I went round to his house, and I said to him, "If I catch you nicking anything, I'll break both your arms or your legs," and I prodded him with two fingers. I've done some boxing and I'm not scared of anybody. I just poked him in the belly, didn't really push him, but he lost his balance and fell over against the door. Nobody was more amazed than I was. He crawled back through the door. The whole community was terrified of him. When this news got round, the whole estate was in an uproar. A few days later, I saw him go into a house. I had the police over and they got him. He went down for nine months. While he was away, I put pressure on his missus to leave the district. She had two partially blind kids, with 80 per cent sight loss. They had chronic rent arrears. This bloke wasn't the father of the kids. I asked her if she was receiving attendance allowance. No, she said, she wasn't entitled. The DHSS had told her, and the local advice centre had confirmed it, that blind people in a secure environment didn't warrant it. So I got this woman to keep a diary of all that she had to do for the children, how often the kids bumped into each other, all the things they couldn't do for themselves. There was on occasion when one of the kids was in the lavatory poohing and the other one came in and pissed all over him. Anyway, in the end, she had the attendance allowance; back-dated it came to nearly £1,000 and each week £31 added to her allowance from social security. The next thing was to get her re-housed; so that would be a way of easing him out when he came out of the nick. You have to make that sort of impact, something that everybody will talk about and remember. That fixes it in the public mind that you mean business. It becomes folklore after a while, but that doesn't do any harm.'

Ken has a mixture of intuitive understanding and of accurate data on the area. He details three kinds of vandalism: for the hell of it, in the furtherance of theft and as a protest against the environment. 'You have to distinguish between them, because they all say something different. When I came here, people were ripping apart their own houses, just to get a move. The only result was that they were living in properties that were even more unfit than they need have been.'

Ken kept a log of some of the humiliations people had to suffer. One woman whose house had no bath or hot water (the system had been taken out before she moved in) was having to bath her children in the kitchen sink; one woman whose toilet was blocked was told by the housing department that she'd have to share with the people next door; in many houses there were no internal doors. In 1981, there had been just 17 official repairs on the whole estate. In 1982, 82 official repairs had been carried out, but in fact the real total was over 900. People began to do their own once some pride had been restored into living here. When it came to allocating the houses, the general feeling was that those who lived here wanted 'better people than us' to come. 'We're all the same here, Ken.' Some people said that they would buy their houses if they were in another part of town, but they wouldn't do so while the stigma of Goscote remained.

The decay of the neighbourhood has been turned around; and in some streets the change is dramatic. In the summer of 1983, there were only five empty properties. Ken has a collection of photographs taken when he first came on to the estate: rubble inside and outside the houses, burnt-out shells, lavatories torn out, heaps of filth and garbage, gardens that were simply mountains of metal and junk. The gardens in some places had merged into a kind of overgrown field. 'It's still a priority estate. The sad thing is that you can't bring about this sort of change just by conventional methods, by adhering strictly to regulations. You can see what conventional management of the estate has done for it over a period of 40 years. It had failed hopelessly.'

One of the demands placed on the Neighbourhood Offices is that they are expected to show results. They are conspicuous and always under scrutiny. The fact that results are achieved is not enough; they must be perceived by the people. It isn't enough simply to open an office; there must be a living interaction between the staff and the residents. The estate is in a ward represented by three independent councillors; but in 12 months no more than seven queries had been raised by these councillors from Goscote. The rehabilitation of politicians is also important. This is why the Labour Party made no wild promises and undertook to do only what it had said it would do in the manifesto.

On the wall of the office is a typewritten notice, headed 'Domestic Violence, Magistrates' Court Act' and going on: '(1) County Court Injuction: No violence needs to be done; (2) Magistrates' Court Injuction: Likelihood of violence that may be committed.' That this should be one of the most prominent notices on display is a measure of the breakdown on the conventional idea of family in many poor parts of the cities.

Typical of the fragility of families were Derek and Sheila, who had been in their new house only a few months before they split up. Sheila is 25, Derek 23. Derek has been unemployed for three years. There are four children; Sheila has a boy and a girl from her first marriage. She had been married to a worker in a hostel for homeless single people in Birmingham and had met Derek there. Her own marriage was already failing at that time. Derek was on drugs, he drank heavily. Unloved by his own parents, he had left home and drifted; he was at that time scruffy, dirty and had been sleeping rough. He says that Sheila transformed him. He had gone into the hostel after an unsuccessful suicide attempt with a breadknife. Sheila looked after him; mothered him in a way. He had felt a sense of security with her. She had told him what to do and he had done it. That was what he had needed at the time. Now, he felt, he had developed. He wanted to move on, have new experiences, meet different people. He felt self-confident and no longer needed what he began to see as Sheila's nagging, her bossiness. She said her feelings hadn't changed. She still wanted him, but she wanted him to be the way he had been when she met him. Derek had met a woman in her late thirties in the estate. She offered him excitement rather than security.

They had lived in two rooms when they first came to Walsall. They were re-housed soon after their second child was born. With the birth of their first child, their relationship had cooled; now, with the second – a boy this time – it had soured. Sheila had put on weight which she couldn't lose. He no longer found her attractive. Their sexual relationship deteriorated. This made her unhappy and she ate more. When I met them, they had all the makings of a new comfortable home: they had been given some posters for the children's room – pictures from *Return of the Jedi*, they had a new carpet, some comfortable chairs. It was, as Derek admitted, the first real home he had ever had. He admits his debt to Sheila for all she has done for him. But in the long, empty days of unemployment and a lack of money, there is no shared project between them, nothing but an introspective preoccupation with their own needs; and that is how things so readily fall to pieces. It isn't that Derek is malicious or cruel; and although he loves his children, this isn't enough to keep them together.

When I called on them just before I left Walsall, Derek had gone from the house for the last time. Sheila was telling the children what had happened. She sat on the bed, sobbing, hugging the three-year-old to her, rocking to and fro and saying, 'Daddy doesn't love us any more, Daddy doesn't love us any more.' The little girl looked at me and said, 'Mummy is poorly.' Sheila has friends in the neighbourhood, but they aren't real supports – people to gossip with, to talk to, maybe, but from whom you can't really expect anything. She was preparing to take the children back to Birmingham, perhaps look for her first husband, or leave them with her mother while she finds a job.

Ken says that this estate has been his life. At the moment he is with a woman from the estate. Her husband had left her, but was threatening to come back, and she was afraid of him. 'I slept there a few nights on the sofa like, to protect her. It all began in the course of duty. One night, he comes with three of his mates, carrying hammers to do me over. I don't ask any questions, just open the door, put one on him hard, before he has time to wonder what's happened. They all scarper. But, needless to say, the authority isn't all that happy about me being with a girl from the estate. It was even suggested to me that I might resign over it. "The public has a right to expect the proper sort of behaviour from neighbourhood officers" sort of thing. But I wasn't married to anybody else, I wasn't breaking the law. They can get lost. If you're going to be in the community, that means living there, taking part in it. Not working in one place and living somewhere else. Not being a commuter.'

I asked Ken how the vetting procedure works for people who

apply for one of the houses here. 'They have to come to a Tenants' Association meeting. I get the names and talk it over with the chairman first, and the committee. If they're known and somebody says, "No way, he used to beat his kids or cause a lot of bother with the neighbours," then we'll be guided by that. There are still one or two families I want off the estate; even though even with bad families, there's nearly always two or three who are OK. You've got to expect to carry some who are wrong'uns, some who are weak and not very bright. But it's a question of balance.'

In April 1983, a family who had been in private housing were re-housed in Goscote. They hadn't been able to keep up the mortgage payments and their house had been repossessed. They had been in Goscote only a few days, when one of the children, a boy of five, fell in the canal and was drowned. There was a collection made all round the estate, although nobody knew the family. The collection paid for the funeral. The general feeling was that, in most places, people would not have been so good; the family would have been left alone with their private grief. But the neighbours busied themselves, kept everyone occupied and helped them through the most harrowing days after their loss. On the day of the funeral, everybody turned out. They had all drawn their curtains, even in the poorest houses; everybody came out and lined the streets; it was an occasion of a quiet and impressive dignity. One woman said, 'It was a tragedy which we all felt. You could see it happening to your own child, It makes you realize how easily it could have been one of ours. You moan at your kids, I'm always on at mine, but it's because you love them. You don't realize until something like this happens how precious they are to you. But I think Goscote showed them that we do understand, there is some caring left in the world.'

Mrs Smith is an energetic and long-standing member of the Residents' Association. She was one of the handful who were working for the estate even through the unpromising years when there was little enthusiasm and morale had reached its lowest point. Through their persistence, they did have some successes, but at that time they had neither the active support of the people, nor the backing of the Neighbourhood Offices. Mrs Smith had her triumphs, but even she had been worn down by the long years of disappointment and indifference. She was herself considering application for a transfer to leave the estate. She works in a factory, assembling car lights; but in spite of her long hours at work, she has always been at pains to show what can be done with the houses when they are properly looked after and maintained. Hers has always stood out, even when all those around were run-down and neglected. It is comfortably furnished; the garden is ablaze in early May with tulips, forget-me-nots, scented gilly-flowers. Mrs Smith says that, a few years ago, she and her husband could never go out together. They had to go out separately, because there was always someone watching the houses for when they were unoccupied. Any house that was known to be empty would be broken into, the meters done at the very least, at worst the whole furnishings and fittings removed – even in daylight.

She says that it was a nightmare when she first started trying to get things done, some of the nuisances removed, some of the mess cleared up, some of the unofficial junkyards regulated. There were threatening phone calls, promises that she would get her windows put in, that her house would be fire-bombed. It is difficult for people who have not lived on the poorest estates to realize to what extent they can be controlled by the strongest who live there; there are districts that are almost no-go areas, in which the police can do very little, because of the silence that surrounds everything that goes on. The ruling villains have imposed their will on the residents; and the fear of reprisals is the most effective form of control. After all, the people who live here have nowhere else to go; the police at best can maintain an intermittent presence. Sometimes there may be anonymous denunciations by neighbours. What many of the poorest communities lack are the leaders who will create an alternative atmosphere to the bullying and intimidation – so many of those who might have helped raise confidence have long departed. What happens is the reverse of solidarity – a resentful silence, where secret grassing to the Social seems the only intervention likely to provoke any response from the authorities. That has changed now. But it does show what pressures were brought to bear on Mrs Smith and those who did remain, out of loyalty, for a principle, because they had hope or wanted to stand by the people whose lives were shadowed by these things.

'People used to say to me, "Why do you live there?" It was a common thing to hear people say, "I wouldn't live in Goscote rent-free." People I used to talk to at work couldn't understand what it was that made me stay here. You don't want to let people down in a way, you don't want to admit defeat. Because it is defeat, if you get out and leave the place to its fate. Why should you?

'We did succeed in getting urban aid in 1979. Even then we were asking for intensive housing management based on the estate. That we didn't get. But whatever happens, even if every house and garden gets rehabilitated, we still shan't be satisfied. It isn't just the physical appearance of the place, although that is essential. It's the feeling of people for each other that counts. If anything, I've increased my effort on the estate since last year, because I've needed to do something since my husband died last July. He died on our thirty-fifth wedding anniversary. And because we had spent so many happy years here, I felt the best thing I could do was devote myself even more to the improvements we'd been working for on the estate.

'My husband had cancer of the lung and throat. He went down from 12 stone to four stone. I nursed him day and night. And, you know, all that time, you never really sleep properly, because you're listening all the time, you're straining for the least little sound. I wouldn't take sleeping tablets. They took him to the hospital only two or three days before he died; and when I went to see him, I said, "Shall I take you home?" He said, no, he'd be all right. The next day, they rang to say he was worse; then by the time I got there, he was dead . . . And his sister died on the same day. And I'd always promised that we'd have his father here and look after him when he couldn't manage any longer; so I had him here and he died a few weeks later; and then my mother went at Christmas. I've had four blows, one after the other. You have to force yourself to carry on and that's what I've done. We both worked our utmost for the community, so the greatest service I can do to my husband's memory is to carry on. That's what it means in the end: you live your life to the full, as intensely as you can, but it doesn't stop there. The love you have for an individual can reach out and embrace everybody in the neighbourhood.

'I started really in 1979. Lack of repairs was what first got me going. There were only two of us at the beginning, myself and one other woman. We went round to some of the neighbours and we found there were some people with up to a dozen repairs outstanding; one or two had up to 18. Quite big things. They had been waiting years. The local councillor suggested we should form a committee, which we did. We had the housing manager come to a public meeting. The hall was full, which in itself was an achievement. He listened to the people's grumbles and we formed the Goscote Residents' Association Committee. We had a lot of meetings, we saw all the various options, the plans that had been drawn up for the area. We were allocated some money to improve the houses, but it was never finished because of a mixture of cutbacks and pilfering, so that fell through and fizzled out.

'We were appalled. We complained to the Ombudsman. They visited the estate and were shocked by what they saw. Even so, we lost. They wouldn't blame the council for negligence. The Ombudsman did say that he thought Walsall council could do something about the dereliction. We got a lot of publicity, the newspapers, ATV. Then, a few days later, the council announced that there would be more money available after all, enough to complete one section of the estate. But we knew that, once they had begun, they would never be able to do just one bit of it, then leave all the rest. It's funny – after the adverse publicity, money mysteriously becomes available. But the estate had come to such a condition that when one of our tenants complained about a missing door, the area superintendent told him to go and take one off a void property. When the authority gets to that stage, you know things really have reached rock bottom. Our aim now is to make this one of the best estates in Walsall.'

Everyone on the estate confirms the feeling of the place being much improved. Grace, a warm-hearted woman in her mid-fifties, has lived here since she was a young woman. Her house is warm and cluttered, lived in and full of children. Three of her grandchildren are playing rummy on the settee. Another grandchild arrives with her friend. Grace asks them if they've had their tea. She has been in this house only a few years: she moved here when her boyfriend died. She had lived with him for 36 years after she left her husband. She has reared two of her grandchildren from when they were only a few months old. She was one of the first to move back into this part of the estate after the renovations had been carried out. Now, it is cared for and well tended; the spring flowers bright in the sunshine; the doors painted, ornaments – glass fish, pampas grass – in the front windows. This is right at the heart of the estate – and, when Grace moved in, all the houses around her were still empty. 'It was the sort of place that nobody visited; not even creditors – and they'll go bloody anywhere. It was a ghost town; a thieves' paradise. The people living round here are good people. I've always been a bit rough. I was in prison a fair bit when I was younger, but the neighbours on the estate always looked after my kids for me. I had three by my chap; they're all married now. They never had to go away while I was inside; and that tells you more about the people round here than the state of the buildings can. It's what's in people's hearts that counts. You've got to look after kids. The only thing I hate is anyone who mistreats kids. They've got to be free to play, you've got to give them room to grow up. The only thing is, I hope snobs don't move into this estate. There's a couple over there, they fetched the police to a six-year-old last week. A six-year-old. I ask you. It's ridiculous.'

Some of the older people on the estate won't be moved out, even for the sake of improvements. George is in his seventies. He lives in a bungalow with his dogs – nobody is quite sure how many – four or five. The inner door is filthy and much of the interior has been fouled by the animals. George wears a woollen cardigan, brown with wear and grime at the front, fawn trousers that bag down from the waist, where they are tied with string, old slippers. He is completely deaf. He has a hearing aid, but doesn't want to use it. He has no particular wish to hear anything anybody might say. This doesn't stop him from talking, though and is quite ready to talk to anyone who will stop and listen. He returns to what was obviously one of the most important and traumatic experiences of his life: he describes how, at El Alamein, he saw 18 of his comrades killed when they were attacked from the air. When he came home from the war, he had a tatting business – scrap metal – which he sold to a relative when he could no longer keep it going. The relative now pays the rent on his house. After the war experience, everything else seems almost trivial; he even tells the story of how his wife died by fire almost casually. 'She was smoking in bed. We only had a mattress on the floor. I only went out to get a bottle of stout and some fags. I stopped for one little drink, that was all. When I was going home, I was met by the coppers. The house was all afire. She was dead.'

There seem to be so many of these stories in poor districts: there are more accidents, more children die, there is a lower life expectancy. It is impossible to spend time in these places and not to appreciate how unfair a society it is that heaps praise upon the clever and successful and rich for their achievements, when the people against whom they have competed struggle under such multiple disadvantages.

Not far away is a family with a son of 14 who is disabled. He had a car accident when he was six and he remains paralysed down one side. His mother was a single parent when the accident happened, with three other children. She couldn't cope with his needs then and he went away to school in Birmingham. She wasn't happy that he should go away at all; and her misgivings were confirmed by his lack of progress. He had been able to walk with help before he went away; now he cannot walk at all. His mother married again and she and her husband fought for two years to get him returned home. They were advised that it was better for him to stay at school. His mother says that he went there to be an ornament – to sit in the corner and be looked at. She feels that he vegetated there, lost the use of his muscles. She feels that it was partly her fault, for allowing him to be parted from her. She was eventually allowed to have him back home; and the house has been adapted to accommodate him. The doorways have been widened to allow the wheelchair to pass; and a lift has been installed in a corner of the living-room to take him upstairs. The lift is a sort of platform that can be raised and lowered. If the boy's arm or foot should get caught, the lift can be stopped by pressing a button. The cost of installation was £17,000. In order to get approval for it, there had to be a little judicious juggling with the accounts. An invoice was put in for some plastering work on non-existent houses. Although there should be no question about limiting the adaptations that should be available to the disabled, there are limits – especially with all the cuts and limits that have been imposed on the local authorities in recent years. In any case, it is far cheaper for the boy to be maintained at home than in a school or hospital. 'When they talk about cuts, this is what it comes down to – a mother having to lift a 14-year-old up and down, take him to the toilet, do everything for him. Cuts sound nice and clean and surgical; what it means is wear and tear on people's lives, using up their strength to do work that is really beyond their power. Those who talk about the country not being able to afford it should be made to live with someone severely handicapped for a month. But even that wouldn't do any good – they'd have to live with someone they love who is severely handicapped for them to get the message . . . The rich don't run the same risks as the poor. Their kids are likely to be more sheltered, they're less likely to get run over, they're less likely to get inadequate medical care, they're less likely to be worn out at 50 with manual work and looking after their family.'

Mrs Kay is pleased to have her boy back home. 'He can talk a bit. We can understand what he says, but outsiders would find it difficult to follow. But you feel bad about leaving him in a place where you can see hin deteriorating. You want to look after your own; only it seems they make it an obstacle course, they put too many things in your way to deter you.'

Next door is one of the few houses boarded up. An old man lay dead here for three days over Christmas and nobody knew about it. There is brown hardboard at the windows. Next to that an immacuately kept house – garden planted with early summer flowers, pansies, lobelia, candytuft. The lawn has been cropped in strips, smooth as velvet. Here lives a man of 99 with his daughter. The old man was a miner, very strict, very much boss of the family as so many of the Victorian working class were. He had a stroke a year ago. His daughter has looked after him; she is a pleasant and kindly woman, but pale and extinguished, She is almost like someone from another age, the woman who effaces herself completely in the service of a parent, of whom she is half-afraid, upon whom she remains emotionally and financially dependent. The old man has bought his own house. He has been proud of this achievement that would have been unthinkable when he started work in the pit in 1896 when the colliers of the West Midlands were still thought of as halfwild, uncivilized, living on the stone flags, wooden chairs and straw mattresses of colliery-owned houses, living their dark and mysterious life in a twilight that repelled and frightened the middle class.

It isn't easy to transform these places that are pursued by their reputation. For one thing, it is expensive to live in poor districts. Basic foodstuffs cost more because there are no shops within walking distance. This afternoon, the mobile shop is stationed in the road. It is a red van with a metal grille over the windows: stacked with sliced bread, tins of vegetables, tins of spaghetti, sweets, cereals, washing powder, biscuits. Women come out to the van. Everything costs more; but the return fare to town on the bus is 64 pence. Many people buy their clothes from the club-man. Some people rarely go to the shops in town – what would be the point, they can't afford anything in them. But this means they have no opportunity to compare prices. I met one woman who had bought a pair of jeans from the club-man for £22 when they were on sale in the town centre for £7. Many people use catalogues and mail order for things – children's shoes, a winter coat, even a cassette recorder or a new carpet. It is always more expensive, but less humiliating than going into the big stores in town and being refused hire purchase because of their address. Some of the insurance companies won't collect on the estate; people's policies run out without them realizing it. Many people are at the mercy of tally-men and moneylenders. And this isn't the limit of the disadvantage. It is sometimes impossible to recruit people sufficiently committed – or even honest – to carry out the public services. On one estate, the warden of one of the old people's sheltered housing schemes was found to be taking money from some of the old people, charging them £1 a time to go shopping.

She had borrowed £300 from one bedridden old woman, which was never returned. Her sons stole purses and extorted money for services; the pensioners were, not surprisingly, afraid to tell anyone what was happening.

The new tenants who have moved into the area in the past three or four years say something about the nature of the recession of the 1980s. There have been quite a few single men (many of them separated from their families by unemployment and the subsequent breakdown of their marriage), who have been prepared to put some work and effort into redeeming the houses from neglect. There are a number of families who have been unable to maintain mortgage payments on private houses, whether because of unemployment or bankruptcy. A few have returned from Canada or Australia, where they went to start a new life and found instead one that resembled too closely the life they were fleeing. A couple of families were the former tenants of pubs, where managers have been installed in their place. Altogether, these are people considerably different from those who have traditionally lived here; and this has coincided with the efforts to improve the neighbourhood, in ways that are clearly discernible.

Ron is in his mid-forties; Jackie, his wife, a few years younger. They have two children – a boy of 19, who has an apprenticeship with GEC in Lichfield, and a girl of 11, whose ambition it is to become a dancer. At first sight, their progression through different kinds of housing looks like a very dramatic example of people who have come down in the world. In fact, it would be the worst nightmare imaginable to most people who are buying their homes and worrying about the mortgage repayments.

Ron and Jackie went from a secluded fourteenth-century cottage in the Staffordshire countryside into a private house on a new estate, and from there to the council house they now occupy in Goscote, on what has always been regarded as the worst estate in Walsall. It is the kind of prospect that would make many people striving to better themselves seriously consider suicide.

But instead of being bitter and unhappy at their fate, Ron and Jackie exude a sense of relief; even of liberation. This is true especially of Jackie. Ron, who has been out of work for 16 months, feels that time hangs heavy and is anxious about the chance of ever working again. But apart from that, neither feels any regret about what has happened. They don't feel resentment or anger at the loss of all they had built up, but rather a thankfulness that they are still together and that the corrosive fear about where the money was going to come from has been lifted.

For 18 years, Ron was a representative for a firm specializing in precision engineering. For a long time, he had been intending to start up on his own, using the contacts he had built up over many years. But he had the misfortune to open his business in 1980. He employed three or four people but was severely under-capitalized. As the recession intensified and interest rates rose, he had to reduce the business to himself and one employee. But the bills still couldn't be paid; the time-lag between production, delivery and payment became too great. The firm went into liquidation in early 1982.

Jackie: 'The worst part of the whole thing was trying to keep the house going on the new estate. That was the most frightening time. We knew the money wasn't coming in, it was impossible to borrow any more. There was a period when I was trying to make do with £10 a week for food for four of us. The mortgage was £225 a month. It was all out of proportion. It was horrible. Here, I'm paying £20 a week for rent and rates. And on that estate, you were isolated. You felt you were alone with your worries. We finished up after 18 months there knowing about three people; and one of those we knew before we even went there. It was one of those places where everybody was out until late in the evening, frantically working away to pay the mortgage on a place they hardly ever saw; milk going sour on the doorstep, dwarf conifers in the gardens which they had no time to cultivate properly; an expensive dormitory.

'Since we've been here, I feel a terrible burden has slipped from us. Ron said to me last night – I was laughing over something quite silly – and he said, "It's good to hear you laugh again." Because I hadn't, I hadn't even smiled from 18 months. He said, "We're getting back like we were." I can't tell you the strain it put on us.'

Jackie loves the house. The window is a clear picture window, which gives a view of the old people's bungalows opposite. You can see the life of the street: the son of one of the old women calls and brings his mother her dinner; the girl next door walks by with her baby and waves. Jackie doesn't want net curtains at the window.

There is some furniture salvaged from the old house – a brocade three-piece suite, a nest of tables. Ron's mother has helped them with the new carpet for the front room. Jackie is houseproud. 'I even go out and wash down the window ledge. People think that's a bit strange – they're not used to doing that round here. Perhaps it'll start a new trend. I've never lived on a council estate before. I'd never thought about it. It had never occurred to me that I ever would. This place had a reputation. You can't live in Walsall and be unaware of it. We were a bit doubtful about taking it at first. But it's been the best thing that has happened to us in years. It's helped us to keep our sanity. The people here are the salt of the earth. The girl next door, she has a baby of seven months and she said she was dubious about accepting the house up here. She said the day she came to view it, I happened to be outside and we had a little chat. She said that was what clinched it for her. They were living in bad conditions, over a tumbledown shop. We've become good friends. I don't regret anything.' They agree that if they had done this 10 years ago, it would have saved them a great deal of worry and anguish.

That isn't to say Ron is happy, being out of work. He has done nothing but apply for jobs. He is always being told that he is too old: he was 47 the day before I spoke to him. Around the room are his birthday cards: joke cards, a Snoopy card, a big affectionate one from his wife. Jackie says they had nothing when they came here. She lost her job at the same time as the business went into liquidation. She was working as private secretary for a firm which did limited edition prints of lesser-known Victorian paintings. One or two of these are on the wall of the living-room: a picture of a little girl in disgrace, standing in a corner with a look of shame on her face, while a collie dog looks up at her beseechingly; a print of a cardinal playing chess with some attendants in eighteenth-century dress.

'It isn't easy, even now. I have to think, every penny I spend.

People get used to living up to a high income and, if you lose it, it terrifies them. But we can see some positive things. Kevin has been offered a permanent job at GEC and he hasn't even finished his apprenticeship yet. That's one bright spot in our lives. Fortunately, I can manage. I enjoy cooking. I used to do catering – just for friends, nothing official; as a pastrycook I'm quite good. I can make a meal out of very little – a few bits of bacon and they'll go into a quiche, a cheap piece of meat can easily be eked out in a hotpot. We haven't eaten steak for months. I shop around for food. I have to watch everything. Even a pair of tights, I have to think, can we afford it?'

The great gain in their position has been that it has brought them closer together. When they were going through all the anxiety about whether they would be able to keep the house or not, they found themselves being driven further and further apart. It came to the point where they could easily have broken up. People unite against poverty, but they break against money. 'One thing it does teach you, is that all the struggle and the striving, the effort and worry – it's all for each other. But you actually lose sight of that when you're in the middle of it. You easily forget it's really all in aid of doing the best for the people you love. But it sort of takes off on its own. You just go along with it and it's controlling you instead of serving you. We don't stop to think, Well, what's it all for? If we did, we wouldn't get into such terrible situations.'

Ron was brought up in a council house. His mother lives over in Shakespeare Crescent. He goes over in the car to fetch her for dinner. He is a corpulent man, with silver hair and a warm smile that transforms his face. He has been deeply affected by the experience they have lived through. He has begun to doubt that he will ever find another job. He feels that he ought to be contributing more to the household. The role of male breadwinner dies hard: that was the essence of the old working-class society and it cannot be set aside just like that. Ron and Jackie are grateful to Ron's mother. She has helped them with basic necessities for the new house. She says simply, 'What else would I have done with my money? There's nothing I want. I play Bingo but that's my only real pleasure; it's better than sitting in a pub with somebody else's husband, isn't it?' Ron says, 'I don't drink or smoke. But I swear. If I didn't do that, I don't know . . .' He agrees with Jackie that getting this house was the best day's work they ever did. 'We did hesitate. People told us that if anything wasn't nailed down or screwed to the floor, it would disappear . . . But I think we're going to be lucky here. I've been digging the front garden. First thing I turned over was a gold ring. It was worth £80.'

Ron and Jackie's story is like an heretical morality play in this society. To have come down so swiftly and to feel, not a sense of failure and shame, but one of release has a pleasantly subversive quality. It shows that it is possible for people to get out of the rat-race – and that to do so, if the alternative is places like Goscote, isn't necessarily a catastrophe. They give a glimpse of the terrible unfreedoms that pass for emancipation in this society: being tied to the money-go-round is a product of fear, the terror of loss as much of positive choice.

At the bus-stop stands a woman in her sixties, neat, tidy grey hair, fawn raincoat with brown lapels; she is carrying a shopping bag. She looks out from the vandalized bus shelter with its buckled roof at the rain. 'Just what we need,' she says. It has been raining every day for two months. Behind her, an old man, sunken eyes, flat cap, silvery stubble on his cheek, an old raincoat that almost sweeps the ground; thin and spectral. The woman is talking, half to him, half to me – to anyone who will listen. Her theme is how much worse everything is getting; that this lament should persist, in spite of the obvious untruth of it, is a measure of people's *feeling*. It has been one of the most glaring failures of the labour movement that it should have disregarded this for so many years. 'We shall have it like it was in the thirties,' the old man says. 'The means test. They even wanted the wedding ring off your wife's finger. She had arthritis, her knuckles was all swollen. "Never mind, we'll cut it off." "What, her bloody finger?" "No, the ring".' 'Oh, I had all that,' says the woman; and creases of bitterness form around her mouth.

A girl with a baby in a push-chair; peach-coloured make-up, cheeks almost orange, hair bleached at the front, fair at the back. I help her on to the bus with the push-chair and a bag of baby clothes she has been to collect from her mother. She is a beautiful child. 'What's her name?' 'Wynette.' 'Oh, where does that come from?' 'Tammy Wynette.' 'I though that was a second name.' 'It is, but I just liked the sound of it.'

Mike comes from County Durham. He is another single man who was allocated a three-bedroom house on the estate because he was prepared to redecorate and carry out some of the minor repairs. He was living with his brother but the brother has two girls and they were getting to an age where they needed the spare bedroom and Mike felt awkward in the house. At the time, Mike was doing three full-time jobs: foundry in the day-time, night shift in a factory and working on the fish market on Saturdays. He is one of those men who are proud of their physical strength and are unhappy if they're not using it. He has lost all three jobs, which was a blow to his pride. He insists on his toughness, how he has maintained his body in good shape. He hasn't let himself go, as a lot of men do when they stop working. He has been unemployed for two years now. When he first came to the estate, the house was in a ruinous condition, the garden overgrown and full of rubbish – bricks, bottles, furniture, rust saucepans, tins, concrete, metal. Mike wears an old corduroy cap, white trousers, sports coat. He rides a Chopper bike, which he assembled himself out of discarded parts. His kitchen is full of bicycle frames, wheels, handlebars, pots of paint, bicycle chains. He repairs and reconditions bikes for people in the neighbourhood – mainly children's bikes; an unofficial and not very rewarding job that might bring in a few pounds from time to time but which at least provides an occupation. He has taken his time over decorating the house; he works very thoroughly, with the result that the value of the house is much enhanced by his labour. The living-room is finished and he has installed units in the kitchen, even though the furniture is sparse and the house has that curious bleakness of places where men live alone. There are no carpets; there is something that suggests helplessness in the accumulation of milk bottles, Nescafe jars, and dirty dishes; the clothes left in the blue plastic launderette bag. There is a buff-coloured suite covered with rexine in the front room, a bare lightbulb. In the garden Mike has built a pond for cold-water fish; at the back, pigeon pens that look as if they have been made of wood retrieved from rubbish-tips. Mike is constructing an aviary with fine mesh wire. He plans to breed budgerigars to make a little extra money. There has always been a tradition of pigeons, avaries, song-birds in the West Midlands.

In the homes of single men there is often a slightly rancid smell of loneliness. Mike is not married. He can live as he pleases and can't blame anyone else for the mess he gets into. He has a terrible temper and would only take it out on anyone he lived with. Like this, he says, 'I can do as I like and have only myself to blame when things go wrong.'

In the old people's flats, lives Maudie Tillett; a woman of 85, ailing but as sharp as a needle, welcoming company and conversation. 'Not before half past ten, though, I haven't got me wits about me till then, what with all these tablets.' She sits in her old-fashioned armchair, with a box of Dairy Assortment on the table beside her, her little plastic phials of tablets in order on the mantelpiece. She has been a formidable woman, a working-class matriarch, utterly dependable and unafraid of anything; but she has lost a lot of weight now and walks with a tubular steel frame with rubber caps at the base. Hers is a story of poverty and rejection by her parents. Although the social experience of her generation sounds alien to young people, the feelings are the same in many ways – unemployment, exploitative work.

Maudie has lived in Goscote since 1937. Her mind is still clear and that, she says, is a great blessing. Even if she can't do what she once could, she still has command over her understanding. 'I've seen this estate right from the time it was first built. It was poor when we first came, some of the people were a bit rough, but there wasn't the vandalism. That only started really about 15 or 20 years ago. When we first came, if anybody was ill or having a baby, the neighbours all did what was expected. Nobody was neglected, you all mucked in. You walked in and out of each other's houses and didn't wait to be asked.'

This is a theme so familiar in the old working-class communities that it cannot be dismissed as nostalgia or fantasy; there must be some substance. What Maudie and hundreds of thousands like her are saying is not that they regret the conditions in which they grew up (which had a bitterly unhappy childhood); but that there existed a spirit of resistance to the conditions in which people lived: the neighbours and work-people protected her even against the violence of her own stepfather. One of the sources of the disappointments in all the achievements of Labour in years after the war among those who fought so bravely for the welfare state and the health services is that no one foresaw the setting up of universal health care and proper social services as a prologue to the caring, to some extent, going out of the daily life of people. Those services were seen as an expression of the caring that already existed in practice, the embodiment of something that was present, in however incomplete and partial a way, in their lives. What nobody imagined was the effect that the welfare state would have once it was set up within a context that was capitalist; the way that relief from insecurity and destitution was the very basis on which the expansion of capitalist society from the 1950s onwards became possible: the growth of the consumer society, all the industries connected with leisure and pop culture, entertainment, fashion, consumer goods would have been unthinkable if the lives of the people had remained shadowed by hunger and disease and want. But these things were marketed with such intensity that they have come to seem the primary reasons for our existence – to the detriment of the caring of human beings for each other.

It has been a slow process of attrition. It didn't happen overnight. Many resistances remain; but over the years, the idea of individual salvation has been slowly replacing the sense of collective struggle: getting on, looking after number one. Even the poorest, those who have least chance of climbing out of the poorest communities, live in the hope of the big win, the lucky number coming up, the prize money, a scoop on the pools. It is one of the bitterest ironies that the institutions which embodied the old collective aspirations of the working class – the trade unions and the Labour Party – still remain but that the feelings which gave rise to them have been eroded. And it is when this very *essence* of solidarity has been undermined that the more overt attack becomes possible: the assault on the unions; the Labour Party appeals to its legions and find that they are invoking an army of ghosts.

It is essential that we understand the processes that are at work and have been at work unsparingly, without pause, even during the moments of greatest prosperity, indeed especially during those periods of prosperity when we have been lulled into believing that capitalism had changed for ever. Solidarity is not something that can be rationalized or modernized: it has only one meaning – the bonding of humanity in opposition to those forces that wish us ill, that wish to keep us in subordination, at their mercy. And those forces remain as they always have been. This is why it is essential to listen to the testimony of Maudie Tillett and those like her – and to know how to listen with an informed understanding, an imagination of the heart and mind. It has nothing to do with nostalgia; but everything to do with the struggle.

4. Building on what we have

Repairing the damage the system does to the people, that's only half the story. The other part is giving the community confidence in itself. All the pride and decency of working people, all the talents that are there, waiting to be used. We have to build on what we have, use what's there. The neighbourhood offices are also to facilitate that self-expression to give people an outlet in the places where they live.
— Brian Powell, leader of the Labour group, Walsall council

Much of the rhetoric about decentralization is about 'giving people control over their lives', mostly in pious generalizations (and indeed, the term 'giving' implies at best a leashed and limited control). The neighbourhood idea goes much further. It aims to build on the resources and abilities that exist in the communities, to act as a focus for people's own strengths which, for the most part, are not called forth by the great concentrations of power and wealth that dominate our lives. It is a question of inspiring confidence where it has been eroded, of reflecting and supporting the values and defences of working-class people which have been under such sustained attack over the years.

There is always a danger of seeing the working class simply as victims; indeed, when you look at the unassailable power of money over the lives of us all, it does sometimes seem easier to accept. This feeling is best exemplified by the old woman who said, 'Even in the 1930s, poor as we were, you could still go and scavenge for coal; you could burn wood, you could even throw old shoes on the fire; if you were desperate, you could chop the legs off the kitchen chair. But what can you do with a bloody gas bill? Pay it, or go cold. So how are we more free now than we were then?'

But the strengths and resistances are still there. It is easy for the pride and the confidence of working people to be submerged by the noise and show from the media, to be drowned out by the clamour of capitalist selling. Indeed, unless this were so, the transformation brought about in Goscote could not have happened at all. Despite the very real erosion of solidarity in the post-war years there are still firm foundations on which the regeneration of community can be based. The neighbourhood idea aims at retrieving those strengths, and building on them, in ways that make the bland phrases about 'taking control of our lives' have real meaning and force in the world. But to perceive these strengths one needs the patience – and the willingness – to listen.

The Sneyd is on the Mossley estate; set apart from the houses, because it was originally a canal pub, serving the barges that took coal from Cannock into Birmingham. The canal has been long filled in and the pub remains isolated, old-fashioned, unmodernized.

By half past nine on a Friday night, there is scarcely a seat left, even though there are padded red leatherette benches round the walls and 20 or 30 stools around the black-top wooden tables. Old-fashioned metal heaters frost windows with condensation. At one table in the socialist half of the pub there are eight or 10 people, mostly men, varying in age from their twenties to Connie who is over 70. The discussion in this place is always political and would not disgrace an academic common room; only it's much more intelligible and funnier. It has the bitter-sweet flavour of working-class experience, with its intertwining of the comic with the tragic, the wry humour and scepticism that haven't been corrupted by cynicism, the tolerance that hasn't been turned into indifference. This is one of the few pubs in Walsall where the 'Red Flag' sometimes get sung at the end of an evening; and where political passion has a meaning that is almost completely absent from those who claim that their business is with politics.

Earlier in the day we had been to Darlaston; one of the most blighted areas of the West Midlands, where one of the greatest concentrations of industry has been transformed into acres of crumbling brick, twisted metal and broken glass and an eerie silence has replaced the thud of machinery. Several of the men worked in Darlaston; At GKB, Rubery Owen. The conversation turns to when they'd been at work.

'When we worked there, the road was thick with bikes. You couldn't move for the traffic.' Now, there is only a scattering of vehicles, the traffic moves freely. But it is only now that so many of the works have closed that some of the stories can be told of how things were – all the fiddles, the day-to-day defences of the workers against the grinding monotony of the work, all the ingenuity that went into making working life tolerable.

'When I worked there, I remember I had a picture of Harold Wilson up on my locker. It was the time of the 1964 election. God knows why I'd got him up. But Princess Margaret was visting the works. They said, "Take that picture down." I said, "No, why should I? It's my personal locker." So they said all right, to leave it. Next morning, somebody had been and ripped it down. Right. We had half a day's strike over that. They had to let me put it back, otherwise the royal visitor would have had the factory to herself.'

'At Rubery Owen's you always felt you were safe. My Dad worked there 30 years. He always used to say to us kids "I'll get you on at Owen's. You'll be alright there. Job for life." How many fathers told their kids that?'

'Bloody sad; when it closes down, it makes your parents look fools for advising you to go there.'

'They had faith in the system. Just like we're expected to have now. Put up with all the unemployment, never mind the poverty, it'll be all right in the end. Just trust us.

'Old Owen was all right. He was a typical, paternalistic employer. You weren't badly treated. But he never knew what was going on in the works. He used to drift in occasionally from his palace in Sutton in his Rolls-Royce.'

'At least your employers were flesh and blood then; not anonymous faceless people you can't even talk to.'

'The bloke who owned the metal works where I was used to

come down in his spats and gloves. When he came in, he used to hold a handkerchief in front of his nose because of the metal and the fumes; you couldn't see from one side of the shop to the other. He wouldn't even breathe it in for five minutes, even though we had to live with it all the time.'

'There used to be a lot of fiddles. We had these rows of lavatories and, in the mornings, the smoke coming out of them, like a fire.'

'The lavatories were used for everything – betting, gambling, selling.'

'There was one bloke used to do haircuts in the cubicles, sixpence a time.

'We had this lad, he was a bit backward, used to clean out the toilets. One day, this guy was cutting somebody's hair in one of the cubicles, and the lad heard him say to the bloke whose hair he was cutting, "Turn round, I can't get at you." Well, this lad thought there was some funny business going on, so he got a bucket of water and threw it over them over the top of the cubicle.'

'There was a bloke used to sell all the papers in the factory. Talk about private enterprise.'

'Somebody else specialized in cigarettes.'

'There was a bloke used to sell Durex. Sold them to the youngsters by the dozen. He was a man of about 50. And he had a daughter of 18. One day she said to him, "I'm bringing my boyfriend home tonight." And so they got all ready to welcome her boyfriend, and when he walks in, he's this lad he's sold a load of johnnies to that morning. And what made it worse, he couldn't say a word.'

'They got away with murder then. Those days they used to promote people from the factory floor to management; and as long as the work got done, they used to turn a blind eye. They knew all the dodges, because they'd been through it themselves. It wasn't till the late 1960s that they got these college-trained men in.'

'And some of them had a bloody tough time. They hated the way we used to take the piss out of them.'

'People have always nicked things from the factories. We had one bloke, he used to design trailers. And he got all his materials from work, used to make them in the workshop at the back of his house. Everything he used should have been bits of cars.'

'One chap was taking water-pumps from Rubery's. He got caught and they prosecuted him. He'd been selling these things. He topped himself.'

One of the group, a man in his thirties, is a building worker. He has been unemployed for nearly two years. 'The only way you can get work now in construction is to go self-employed. That way, the big firms don't have the responsibility for putting your insurance stamp on, all the overheads, health and safety, it becomes your problem. Why should I go self-employed? There's no unemployment benefit, you've got no protection. You're on your own. They try to put the pressure on to break the union, that's what it's all about. Kid you that you're independent if you're self-employed – it's a way of smashing the union by the back door and getting labour cheaper. Last time I went to sign on, there's this clerk, younger than me, he sits there and he says, "Isn't it about time you settled down and got a proper job?" A proper job! I can't believe it. "I've been working in construction since I left school 20 years ago." He says, "I know you building workers, all over the place, no settled life, live like gipsies roaming the country." The bloody cheek of it. I've been married 16 years with three kids, I've lived in the same bloody house 10 years. Why should I have to be spoken to like that?

'It's as if everything is deliberately arranged to undermine working-class people, our confidence in ourselves. Like all the architects and engineers on the sites, the number of times they've come to us, the blokes who do the work, when something has gone wrong. They ask your opinion. How should we do this? How could this be put right? How could we change that? Then you'd tell them what you know from years of experience. "Oh no no no, quite impossible." Then they'd go away and write a bloody report and it would say exactly what you'd told them. They'd get all the credit for it. Pick your brains, then be praised for their professional understanding. You're just the ignorant know-nothing workers.'

In the corner of the pub sits a man in his fifties; solitary, bitter; one of the few people drinking alone. His face is grey, his skin the colour of the metal his body has absorbed over the years. He has been a polisher and his working life has been a long slow poisoning. His fingers are shortened by the polishers kicking at the back of his hand every day for so many years. Even though the old industries close down, the firms are taken over, the machinery is dismantled, the men and women who worked in them continue to bear the scars. Long after even the profits have been consumed, the human material remains unhealed and recompense is impossible for what has been done to people.

On the edge of the group sits Connie, now in her seventies. She went into service when she was 14 and, 60 years later, is still working as a cleaner. She says, if all the floors she has scrubbed were placed on end, they would go round the earth. She still gets up at half past five every morning. Widowed seven years ago, she is being courted by two old miners; and their rivalry – more than half serious – is one of the running jokes of the pub. Connie has found a new lease of life through the Neighbourhood Offices. She is selling tickets for a draw in aid of the old people's Christmas Party; once round the pub and her 100 tickets have gone. She is always baking, makes wine and jam and takes it into the Neighbourhood Offices. Today she has brought me a bottle of rhubarb and a bottle of grapefruit wine. She passes round a photograph of herself taken in Jubilee year, playing in goal in the men versus women match on the green in the centre of the estate. In shorts, she is laughing all over her face. The conversation turns, as it almost always does when there are older people there, on the gains and losses that have occurred in working-class life in living memory.

Connie says, 'When we were young, we didn't need much to enjoy ourselves. We'd go out over the fields with a bottle of pop and a jam sandwich, stay out the whole day, never be bored. I used to go out with my mother in the spring, when the dandelions came out, and we'd gather bags full of them. My mother used every part of the dandelions: she dried the root and ground it up into powder for dandelion coffee, you took the young leaves for lettuce, then you gather the flower heads full open at midday to make wine; the old leaves you fed to the rabbits. How many people would know how to do that today? And it never cost us a penny.'

Sam is in his late fifties. He has been made redundant recently and accepts that he will never work again. He says, 'People used to be flesh and bone. Not now. They're made of plastic. Before we shall learn, we shall have to have all the television sets taken away, all the cars swept off the road, we shall have to go back into the gutter, down to rock bottom before we shall learn. We shall have to go back to like it was when I was a lad. We lived at number 2, Number Three Court off Lichfield Street – they never even gave the courts names, just numbers. I was the youngest of eight; four boys and four girls. One room up, one down. We slept, the four boys with our dad in one bed, the four girls with mam in the other. They never had any privacy. I don't know how they went on for their marital life. I often wonder how we were all conceived. They had to go up to bluebell wood. I know one thing, it wasn't in the house, the only times me dad wasn't working he was worn out and sleeping. We had no gas, no electric. Oil-lamps was the only lighting. Her had to cook over the fire. Even so, we weren't the bigest family in the court. There was one with 11 children.

'But your parents always had time for you. They had more time for us than people do now for their kids. They worked longer and harder than anybody does today, they had bigger families, but they always had time to give their babbies. We walked miles with they. Today, people give their kids money instead of time. Everything can be turned into money in this system. Love can become money, time, everything. My dad died, just over 50 he was. Worn out by work.'

We had been to visit Sam earlier in the day; a council house on the main road that runs through the Mossley. In his last workplace, eight men were to have been made redundant. The company had intended to arrange this on a last-in first-out basis. 'But there was youngsters there, blokes with two or three babbies; they knew they'd have a hell of a job finding anything else. Some of them had already had 18 months, two years out of work, they still hadn't paid off the debts they'd got then. I was shop steward. So I went to the gaffer and said, "Why don't you ask for voluntary redundancies? That way, even if you only get four, you won't upset so many people's lives." I said, "You can put my name down for a start." I knew they wanted me out. They said, "Oh well, why not? We'll talk terms." I thought, well, it's the least we can do for the youngsters. Perhaps when they get a bit older, they'll remember, and they might do the same for somebody else.'

Money becomes the subject of the pub conversation.

'Working people are guilty about having it. It's as if they can't get rid of it fast enough.'

'There's no sense in getting used to big money. You only learn to depend on it, then you can't do without it.'

'You just spend what you have. When it's gone, it's like being back to normal.'

'I started work when I was 13 and I got 12s 6d.' (Sam won't use 'new money'; he always interprets prices in pre-decimal values.) 'My Dad was a caster. I started as a caster's labourer. You had to barrow in all the sand, all the materials, run all his errands. I had to cook his breakfast on a shovel in the foundry, every morning, Saturday as well.

'I think we'm got spoiled round here. It was always easy to get a job. If anybody said anything you didn't like, you only had to walk over the road to get took on somewhere else. Even in the 1930s, we had people from Wales and the North coming to the West Midlands. I've walked out of job a dinner-time and started somewhere else in the afternoon. Just like that.

'We thought, didn't we, after 1945, that it had all changed for ever. We grew up to say, "Never again." But here we are, the same old story, all over again.

'What Labour did after the war, we thought that was it. We thought the things we'd achieved could never be taken away.

'The Tories never changed. They just had to bide their time. They were frightened by 1945. But they knew they had to go softly for a few years. That was what the never-had-it-so-good years were all about. Get Labour to drop its guard. The unacceptable face of capitalism had had a bit of plastic surgery. It was still the same bloody face. And that's what we're seeing now.

'We shall have to go back to poverty before some of the buggers'll wake up. Like when we were young: two lavatories down the yard shared between 12 houses, about 80 people. You had to bring the lavatory pan indoors to warm it by the fire, because you couldn't sit on it till you'd melted the bloody ice.'

'You used to go down the yard with a candle and you had to bang on the lavatory door to let the rats know you were coming.

'That's how you can tell who was born in the slums in Walsall. If they've got scars on their arses from the ratbites, they were born on the slums.

'People wouldn't accept going back to that.'

'Wouldn't they? They're accepting it now, them out of work.'

'I don't know. They tell us that work is the be-all and end-all. My Dad finished work on the railways after 45 years. They give him a clock. There he is, cycling home from work on his last day, with this clock in his canvas bag, pleased as Punch. He puts it on the mantelpiece. There. Really proud. He says to me, "That's what you ought to do." He really thinks of it as an achievement. Well, it was in a way, endurance test, getting up at five o'clock every day for 45 years. It's really sad to see it, the humility. People were grateful for the work they were given, as though it was charity.'

'Yes, but you have to think that. You couldn't give up that much of your life and say at the end of it it had all been a load of crap. That's a defensive reaction. The other side of it would be too terrible to contemplate – all those years of your life used up and a clock to tick the last few years away. What a mockery.'

'Yes, and I'll tell you sommat else. The bastards who used to preach to us about the virtue of work and discipline are the same ones who are now preaching to us about the joys of leisure, as long as we take our redundancy money, behave ourselves and keep quiet.'

'By leisure, they mean leisure on their terms – bloody unemployment. Leisure's all right – as long as it's what I want to do – build a boat, go fishing, spend three months out of my life rock-climbing or learning to play a musical instrument. That's all right.

'Yes, but their leisure means selling something to you that's going to fill their pockets. Videos, pornography and tranquillizers because it gets you over-excited. God help us. Our meaning of leisure isn't the same as theirs.'

'Leisure to them means getting money out of you.'

'Money is like a homing pigeon. The working class can't handle it; they let it go and it flies straight back to its rightful owners! It has the homing instinct, knows where it belongs.'

We talk about the Neighbourhood Offices. What difference have they made to the neighbourhood?

'This estate was built in the 1950s; and it's never been a community, not in the sense that some of the others are. But that's changing. We've got part of an old school building, it's been cleaned up and we're already getting it booked up with groups that want to use it – an unemployed people's centre, mother and toddlers, disabled, women's groups, young people, It's as if the estate had been waiting for something to happen for years. That wouldn't have come about without the Neighbourhood Office.'

'To me the Neighbourhood Offices are about democracy. Democracy isn't about going and putting a cross on a piece of paper once every five years, or even once a year if you remember to go and vote in the local elections. It's about being involved in decisions that affect all your life all the time. It isn't good enough to vote once every five years and then sit back and fold your arms moaning about what they do in your name. We shouldn't sit there passively, waiting for other people to do things for us.

'The really good thing about the Neighbourhood Offices is that it starts people asking questions. Not all the people, but some of them. They come in and ask, "Why should we put up with this? Why does the system work like this? Who decides that we can't get these repairs done, who decides the money is going to be spent on one thing rather than another?"

'The Labour Party has been just as bad as the others in this in the past. Just elect us, and we'll sort it all out for you. Without educating people about the limits the system places on them. They talk as though they could do anything for us; the sky's the limit, you know what it's like at election time. Then, of course, they can't do it. Then they wonder why people get cynical.'

'You've got to let people experience how the system works, not make promises that you'll change it. You can't change it, without their back-up, the depth of support of the people. But once you've got that, boy, you can do anything.'

'To a lot of people, capitalism doesn't mean anything. It's the air you breathe. It's just the way we live. They don't even realize that it's just one system, and that it could be changed.'

'I feel sorry for the youngsters. They grow up, some of them have no idea how things work. They come into the office, "Why can't I have a house?" They might have come from outer space for all they know about the society they live in.'

'They'll learn, though. As they get older, can't get work, try to bring up a family, they'll have to go through the same experiences we did. I didn't know much when I was a youngster. I bloody do now. I've had to.'

The evening in the pub has a familiar, almost ritual shape. General chat evolves into political discussion; then as the evening wears on, this gives way to more relaxed anecdotes and stories; then reminiscence and, finally, as people become more relaxed, jokes, laughter, the memory of shared experience. The crescendo of noise increases in the pub. The juke-box is too loud. The landlord is new. 'He'll have to be educated. We come here to talk to each other, not be drowned by that racket.' The smoke coils in bluish wreaths, the beer spills slightly over the tops of the glasses. They tease Connie about her boyfriends. 'Come on, love, make your mind up.' 'No fear,' she says. 'Keep 'em on a string. You get more out of them that way.'

Jim says to Sam suddenly. 'Hey, Sam, what mustn't you on any account do with caviar?' Sam answers immediately, 'Put it on warm toast.' 'That's right.' 'Ruins it, doesn't it?' Both being unemployed, they had been watching the same TV programme at dinner-time. Jim says, 'Who the fuck do they think is watching TV at one o'clock in the afternoon? The unemployed, the old, the house-bound. Hints about how to serve caviar. What a bloody insult. It's like rubbing salt in the wounds.'

There is warmth; laughter. The jokes aren't particularly funny in print. ('You can tell winter's coming, all the blue tits are out.' 'Mind they don't go for your nuts.') But it is the feeling that counts, independently of the words in which it is expressed. Here, you have a strong sense that traditional bonds between people, the power of personal contact, the shared scepticism are a far more potent force than the assaults on the working class by the media and the official opinion-formers, all those attempts to make people doubt themselves and each other, to invalidate their experience, to set their own abilities at small worth. It is the dignity and the pride of people that the neighbourhood idea supports and to which it offers a space to express itself. The people here offer a living example that there is an alternative to the worship of wealth and the disfiguring of humanity that flows from it, which is what the rich propose to us as a model for all our best hopes and dreams.

One of the last Neighbourhood Offices planned was to have opened in Harden just after Labour lost control of the council in May 1982. The opening was cancelled by the new council; and the building has remained on site, empty and unused since then. However, the area is one of the most deprived in Walsall; it was one of the first estates to have been built in the town. A group of local women have been campaigning to get the office opened; or, at least, to have it used as a centre for the community. None of these women had had any previous involvement in politics or local government; theirs was a spontaneous campaign, which has been vigorous and sustained. More than this; it has been for them a considerable educational experience. Their group is a powerful demonstration of just how much resilience there is in working people – especially women – when they are under attack. There's no overt feminist impulse to their campaign; but the feeling is there, below the surface. Not everybody will accept the inevitability of unemployment, poverty and apathy. A few afternoons spent in their company demonstrated the strengths of community more effectively than anything else, as well as the assault on it, not only by the current recession, but by the long-term influences that are always at work, trying to break down resistances, to breach the defences of working people.

Mrs Keach lives in Shakespeare Crescent. Her house lies between two unofficial enterprises run by members of the same family, perhaps best described as a scrap metal and surplus goods business. The houses are red-brick, semi-detached, with square front gardens and facing on to the canal. As you sit in her front room, you can actually see the parallel economy in action. Men push barrows down the street, one full of timber, another carrying two TV sets. Somebody is walking off with council fencing; a sense of constant and vague enterprise takes place, a scavenging and unofficial economy that flourishes outside any official employment structure. It isn't on the scale of significant villainy; but an existence on the margin, a finders-keepers morality, in which everything that isn't attended must be looking for a home.

It is mid-March. A grey damp afternoon. The estate is deserted, the shiny bitumen reflects the greyness of the sky. The grass on the verges is brown, the concrete lamp-posts wilt in the dingy afternoon. Mrs Keach lives in a four-bedroom house; the red brick is raw as a wound in the failing light; the rose-bushes in the front garden have been cut back to a few thorny shoots; the bulbs have just begun to appear in the muddy earth.

Inside, Mrs Keach has set aside one room where she can escape the constant demands of the family. Her son and daughter, 18 and 20, live at home; both are unemployed. The room has an electric fire, a picture of Jesus on the wall, some country-and-western records besides the old-fashioned record player, a glass-fronted cabinet, stretch-covers on the upright armchairs, a glass table. Mrs Keach is in her mid-fifties and has been a widow for three years. The other women are younger, one in her forties two in their thirties. Although the idea of our conversations was to talk about community, the discussion opens up to embrace the wider questions of the way we live now; and the picture of the estate they give is more telling than any of the official versions. It is an intensely political discussion; but because of the limited range of what we acknowledge to be politics, it may not be recognised as such.

Mrs Keach is an energetic and resilient woman, who doesn't mind being seen in public without her teeth; always laughing, even though, underneath her robustness, there is that appreciation which is often found in older working-class women of the pathos of life, the humour and the tragedy so close together, which created such a distinctive sensibility in her generation, a mixture of generosity, tolerance and humour. Mrs Keach says she has nothing else to lose in life, so she can say what she feels quite freely; she has no one to impress, no one to ingratiate herself with. She has always known trouble and has enough of it at the moment. Her boy, 18, who has the mind of a 15-year-old, is in trouble over his relationship with a 15-year-old schoolgirl. But since what is said to have happened took place at Christmas and went unreported for over three months, there are considerable grounds for doubt. But she is worried about him; he has also been taking money from her purse. He is an introverted young man, looks younger than his age; and he is just far enough behind those of his own age to realize how much cleverer everybody else is. This is a particular kind of torment which those better endowed cannot possibly appreciate.

'Anyway, you know what girls of 15 can be like these days, they're not children at all, are they? Some of them lead the lads on.'

Mrs Keach has rent arrears of several hundred pounds. She won't let her children or grandchildren go without anything. She draws £32.85 widow's pension and takes £12 each from the two youngsters at home. TV costs £2.80 a week. She is paying back £2.50 a week on a loan which she took out for the TV licence. It is almost impossible for the well-to-do to imagine the efforts, the juggling with money that the poorest are expected to be capable of. Thirteen pounds fifty pence goes in rent; now about to be stopped at source from the DHSS. In winter, she pays £7 a week for electricity and about the same for gas. 'I buy cheap meat. I bought four pork chops yesterday, £1.68. I go to market Tuesday for some fish, I get the tail-end of cod, because it's cheapest. I go to Tesco's because I can buy the cheapest loaf in town there, $30\frac{1}{2}$. But it costs 64p on the bus.' She won't go into the local shops, because they are far more expensive.

Mrs Keach earns £6 every Saturday for a cleaning job at the Salvation Army Citadel. Last week, the major, who pays her, was not there. She relies on that money for the weekend food. She had only a pound in her purse. She bought two loaves and some potatoes; that was what they lived on for the weekend, with margarine, Bovril and jam for flavour.

The discussion about maturity of young girls leads them to talk of their contrasting experience of adolescence. 'I knew nothing about sex till I went to work,' says Mrs Keach. 'My mother never told me anything. I was granny-reared; they were a bit old-fashioned. It was in the 1930s. My dad was out of work and my mother found it hard, so I went to my granny. When I had my first boyfriend, I went with him for a few months, till I fell with our Phyllis. I thought he would marry me. I didn't know he was married. And I wouldn't have found that out if I hadn't been in hospital having the baby in the next bed to his wife who was having one as well.

'My mother said when she was a girl her mother asked her if she'd done anything with a boy. She said, "Yes," because he'd kissed her. And there was such a fuss because they thought she might be pregnant. She thought that was what made you pregnant, so she couldn't tell them!'

Although Mrs Keach's life has often been touched by poverty and sadness, she laughs at the ignorant girl she was then. One of her daughters has two brain-damaged children: a boy of 10, whose life expectancy is only a few months. 'They've had a lift put in the house to get him up and downstairs, but of course that costs a fortune in electricity. He can't do a thing, bless him, but just sits rocking to and fro, to and fro. And he's in such pain that he has to be in a cradle all the time. His brain, instead of getting bigger as he grows, is wasting away. He looks terrible, it'd break your heart to see him. And the little girl is blind. They've two other children who are well, thank God, But it almost makes you wish the little boy could be called, his life is such a burden. When he was away at special school, he used to like to sit and watch himself in the mirror. His dad has made him one at home, so he can look at himself.' In these poor estates, there is always a higher incidence than elsewhere of nearly all problems and handicaps; more disablement, more single parents, more mental illness; more suffering. It is against people like these that the rich and successful measure the triumph of their wealth and merit.

Joan is in her late thirties. She has four children. Her husband, a carpenter, has been out of work for 18 months. He is on valium; and, at 42, feels he is useless, is convinced he'll never work again. 'He heard of a chap who was only 35 last week and he was told he was too old for some job he went after; and it wasn't something you think of as a particularly young man's job. He keeps saying, "What hope have I got?" Since he lost his job, he's been ill a lot. I decided I wouldn't work while the kids were young. I was going to wait till they grew up a bit and then start work. I did what Mrs Thatcher says you should do. I stayed at home with them. And now look at us. We've always worked hard, done what we were told is our duty and now look at us. It hurts. It hurts me to see my husband like that. But it makes me angry as well. Those people who rule over our lives, what do they know about it? What can they understand? I've never had to say no so much to my kids as I've had to in the past 18 months. We get £125 a fortnight, £62.50 a week and child allowance £23.'

Chrissie, like Joan, also has three boys and a girl. The oldest boy is leaving school at Easter. The prospect is bleak. 'He'll have to join his father on the dole.' Chrissie doesn't know which one of them will find it the more embarrasing – the father, who has always advised his son and expected him to follow him in his trade, or the son who has always looked up to his father. It's a humiliation for both of them; they feel they can't offer each other what a father and son ought to offer each other. It's at moments like these that you feel how the fabric of working-class life is stretched. Whatever changes occur, they won't be for the benefit of working people, whose dignity is damaged, self-esteem impaired. Even at times of greatest improvement, violence is still done to the lives of people; and the hurt it inflicts has no place in the accounts. Chrissie was working when her husband lost his job, but she had to give it up. 'I was earning £30 a week in the post office; but, with his unemployment benefit, I was allowed to earn just £4 before it started to be taxed. Two of mine are leaving school this year. I shall lose £20 family allowance and some off the unemployment benefit. Of course, they'll get their few quid, but you can't take all that off them; they must have something of their own to spend.'

The talk turns to the neighbourhood. Yesterday, the gas man was attacked as he was emptying the meters on the estate. 'He'd been to two houses, £500 in 50p pieces. Whoever did it followed him, and when the van pulled up, they had him.

'I saw a lot of police cars. I went out. "What's going off?"

"Somebody's done the gas man." "Somebody clobbered him and took off with his bag." Nobody seen anything, even though it was broad daylight, middle of the day.'

'That's it. What you know you daren't say because you're frightened of what they'll do to get their own back on you. Oh, I could tell a story about some of them round here, but it'd be more than my life's worth to stand up in court and say it . . . Middle of the day, everybody blind and deaf.'

'It's not the first time. There was a lad down here snatched the gas man's bag; but he took all the 50p pieces to the post office. Daft thing to do.'

'I know who he was. He used to knock about with one of my boys. Right from a kid, he used to steal things, he'd be down the Co-op taking a packet of biscuits. He once asked Kevin to stand watch for him, but Kevin ran off. And his father was the security guard there.'

'Things that go on round here, it makes Coronation Street look tame. Do you remember that time they got the rent man. Oh, he was a snotty-nosed devil, treated the people like dirt. That day – it went round the estate like wildfire – everybody was saying, "The rent man's been done, the rent man's been done. Damn good job." They were waiting for him at one house, and the woman said, "Would you like to come inside?" And she and her husband and the neighbour grabbed him and tied him up and put him in a bath full of cold water. Trussed him up like a chicken. They did time for it. They must have known they'd never get away with it.'

'He was hated though, that man. There used to be some horrible rent collectors, but he was the worst.'

'I could never steal anything. Once the television man left no end of money on our sideboard by mistake. When I went down and told him, he'd forgotten which house he'd left it at. But I could never take it. We've always told our kids never to get involved in anything dishonest.'

'Once when I was a little girl, I was shopping with our mother in Woolie's and she was buying some seeds for the allotment, peas and beans; and while she was looking at the packets, a whole pile of them slipped off the counter and fell straight into her basket and she didn't notice. Her paid for the packets she wanted and when she got outside and saw what she'd got in her basket, her was horrified.'

'Nowadays there'd 've been a store detective grab her and swear she lifted them.

'When our Simon was little, we came out of Woolworth's one day and he opened his hand and said, "Look, Mummy, spiders." He'd got a fistful of false eyelashes.'

'Yes, Jason came home trailing a string of odd shoes behind him that they'd left on a rack outside the shop.'

'I blame some of the shops though; they do put temptation in people's way.'

'When Linda was younger, she got involved with a girl called Jackie and she was the leader of a gang of kids who went and did organized shoplifting. One day the police rang at the door. They'd got Linda down at the station. These four girls were dab hands at lifting and they'd given Linda the bag to hold, because she wasn't used to it. And she's been caught with this bag full of things. They'd go past the counter, slide things off, then walk round the store and slip it into the bag as they walked past Linda. They let her go, because it was the week her dad died. They let Linda off with a caution. The police knew these other girls. They'd been taking things home for months. The things the police found! One of them had been taking it to her granny's – all sorts of stuff and hidden it under the bed. And the funny part about it was, none of it was any use to them at all, not things they could eat or wear. There were electric toasters, irons, batteries, hardware, scrubbing brushes, tins of spaghetti, anything they could lay their hands on. Why would they take things just for the sake of taking them? But I knew why Linda was doing it. At the time, I was fostering a little boy who lived up the road and who'd been neglected by his mother. She was a case, she was always off all over the place, chasing round after young lads, 17-year-olds. And I took this kiddie. I really loaded him with all the love I'd got, because Linda's father had just died. Linda felt she was being shoved out. I could understand what was upsetting her and put it right. She hasn't been in any trouble since then.'

'There's so many kids not properly looked after. They wander the streets, can you wonder if they get molested. I've seen four and five-year-olds going to the shops late at night, pitch dark.'

'We tried to start a childminding group. Unofficially. We didn't want to do it for money. But social services said we had to have a registered childminder, certificates, they wanted the lot. They made it as awkward as they could. We didn't want to charge for it; all we wanted to do was help out. But we had to give it up in the end.'

'You need something to keep you occupied when you're not working. Especially if you're both at home all day; at the end of the day you've nothing to say to each other. It's a terrible strain. If you've got some other interest, at least you've something to tell. Otherwise, it's just sitting and staring at the television.'

'You look forward to little things, though, things you take for granted when you've got the money. I had a gas rebate from the meter this week and I could go out and buy shoes – trainers for the boys and shoes for the girl. I felt it was a real red-letter day.'

'You don't realize until you haven't got the income just how you come to depend on it. When it stops, it's like a bath of cold water. My husband was a fitter until his job went two year ago. He worked for little private firms, offices, shelving and partitioning. The firm wasn't unionized, but he was getting good money – £150, £160 a week. But since he stopped, it feels like getting old overnight. He does the garden and he's got half of my dad's allotment. He goes fishing, but of course it's the breeding season now, so that finishes until June. But it's not a full-time occupation. He grew a garden full of lettuce last year, I should think the whole estate was eating our lettuce.'

A little later on the conversation shifts to other realities of life on the Harden estate.

'The things you know about people. Only you daren't say anything. You daren't go to court because they'd take their revenge on you. The bloke over there, he's just built a lovely veranda, but all the wood's come from the fencing that was going to be used for the modernization.'

'They left some houses empty near us. Only one day they stood empty. They took the sink unit out, all the copper pipes, the boiler, just left the water gushing. The workmen had left their tools inside, they were nicked as well. They used the burners to break into the house next door, took all the pipes out there too.'

'They'll have all the fittings, toilet, bath.'

'You don't have to interfere. The people next door to me, oh, he was a violent man. He used to knock his wife around. She died and left twins; only babies they were. She died of a brain haemorrhage. He'd set about her only two days before, gave her such a belting. That's what did for her, no two ways about it. Everybody knew. Only nobody said anything. It never came out officially.'

'It's more than you dare do to get involved. You never know how they'll pay you out.'

'But he's a bit loony that one, isn't he? If his pigeons don't win the race, he'll get that mad with them, he'll wring their necks and throw them in the canal. Many a time I've seen the pigeons floating in the water when he gets into a bad mood with them.'

'That's right. They had a bin full of pigeons in the garden a few weeks ago. Mandy came in and said, "They've a dustbin full of pigeons. Next day, it was just feathers. They'd plucked them and ate them."'

'You find all sorts in this canal at the back here. Pigeons without heads, cats and dogs. A settee floated past last week. Looked a good one as well, better than ours.'

'If anybody pinches a car, it finishes up in the canal.'

'Somebody pinched the councillor's motorbike. He came up to see somebody about something, parked it outside the house, when he came out it had gone. His wife sees some kids riding about on it a few days later. "Where did you get that from?" "Found it." "That's my husband's bike." They said they'd bring it back. They did, they left it on his doorstep; only by the time he got it, there was nothing left of it, no engine, no wheels. It had been stripped.'

'I think kids are definitely getting harder, don't you? We never dared disobey. What your parents said went. Your dad was your dad, and his word was law.'

'There isn't the feeling for people there used to be.'

'You have to be hard to survive today.'

'They've moved the old people out of the bungalows. They lived in fear.'

'That old girl that lived in the cottage the other side of the canal, she committed suicide you know. After her husband died. They say she lost the will to live. Just walked into the canal.'

'You could swim in that canal when we were young. It'd poison you now.'

'You'd come out with a lovely suntan. It's orange. The copper works.'

'I came here from Lichfield. Where we lived, they were all army houses and, if anybody was in trouble, everybody would be round to help. But not now. It's different now. The young 'uns, they couldn't care if the whole street was on fire. As long as it didn't affect them, they'd go indoors and shut the door.'

'You don't like to get involved, Especially if there's trouble.'

'Mind you, I think people are crying out for a bit of company and friendship. I know one thing – since we've been campaigning for the community centre, it's altered my life. I feel I've got closer to the people here. We feel we're battling for something. We're going to help Labour at the election, because they'll open the Neighbourhood Office if they get in. We've got Independents in this area now. None of us has had any interest in politics, not until now. When you're working, you're life is so busy, you don't stop to think. But when you look round, you see all the things wrong with the place. But people feel they can't do anything on their own. The secret is getting together.'

'It's different from what it was like in the 1930s. People have it easier, they're not destitute like they were then, but they're not so close either.'

'You feel ashamed if you're not working. You feel you shouldn't be walking about the streets if you're strong and able-bodied. It worries my husband. He's on tablets. We have that many rows. Over nothing. A few months ago, I was ready to divorce him. After 20 years. We've had more arguments since he's been out of work than we've had in all the rest of our life together. Getting to know the people here has been a godsend to me.'

'I know how he feels. I got into such a state that I used to start crying if anybody so much as spoke to me. And, if anybody said anything kind to me, I'd just break down. I used to run to the bathroom and lock myself in.'

'We got to the point where we couldn't speak to each other without starting a row. One night, I went to bed and I thought, this is it, I'm divorcing him. Only then he came in and said he was sorry and it wasn't his fault. It's as if you feel you've nothing to offer each other. When you've no money, it seems you're ready to explode at the least little thing.'

'I used to hate it here. I was looking for a transfer. But since we've got together more, I wouldn't want to move now. Even though there are some terrible people . . . I shouldn't say so really.'

'They were talking of making the old people's bungalows into single people's flats.'

'If they do, they might as well hang red lamps at both ends.'

'Look at that lot on the corner. Gipsies. They came back from a funeral at six o'clock one morning. Drunk.'

'That chap she was living with – JR they called him. They took all his children away because he wasn't a fit person to look after them.'

'Well, that Mrs Pearce, she and her daughter have swapped husbands. With her *daughter*. If you've ever heard anything like it. And she was always the cock of Goscote, you couldn't touch her with a barge pole.'

'Was she the one who had that baby? Her bloke was in the army and he wrapped it up in a sack and put it in the boiler at the barracks?'

'Sergeant went to light the fire one morning and there it was.'

'While they buried that old bloke from the bungalows the other day, the gipsies on that corner were all revving up their cars. The noise they were making, it was wicked, even while the funeral cars stood outside the house . . . At one time, they'd shut all their curtains and people'd stand when a funeral went by. The men used to take off their hats, pay their respects to the dead. Not now.'

'There isn't the respect. Not for people or anything.'

'One woman down here, she was lying in bed one night and it was a wet night; and suddenly she felt this water dripping on her.

She thought, this roof has never leaked. They'd been up on the roof, taking the lead while she slept.'

'I know when we went to Grace's funeral, even in the crematorium, all round the coffin, they'd got these buckets catching the rain, because somebody had stripped the lead from the roof.'

On some estates, there is almost a sense of siege. People feel beleaguered, good generous people, trying to bring up their families in adversity and unemployment. There is a great deal of silent suffering and heroism. In spite of the constant struggle, there remain the resilience and the humour; and, with the women of Shakespeare Crescent, a resolve not to let the community fall into the kind of apathy and indifference that afflict so many of the new estates. 'You don't know whether to laugh or cry'; one minute, they are wiping away the tears of laughter, the next, they fall silent at the pathos of things; and yet, it's all so inextricably mixed. They have the measure of it, a sense of values – the importance of bringing your kids up decent, respect for others, care for the neighbourhood; something well anchored and stable, even though you can feel the strains on the community, and the fabric of life seems sometimes stretched almost to breaking point.

I have a sort of general, composite memory of all the homes I went into in Walsall: a gas fire built into a stone surround, with a mantelpiece ornamented with Staffordshire china chaffinches or a china Victorian couple, a brass vase, behind which are tucked a gas bill and an official communication from the council. On the wall, a brass hunting horn or brass tray, perhaps crossed swords or pistols. On the TV, smiling photographs of a child or grandchildren against an impossibly blue sky. There is often a sofa that is really a bit too big for the small rooms, brocade, leather or velvet covered; a patterned carpet, with a rug in front of the fire; a dresser with ornaments, sporting trophies, carvings of an antelope or elephant in simulated smooth ebony. There might be a multi-coloured glass fish in the window or some pampas grass dyed russet and dark green. On the walls, a painting of a little boy crying glycerine tears or a Constable reproduction; a music centre or a video. The evening paper lies crumbled by the chair; working boots and overalls in the kitchen. The homes of the older people are slightly less comfortable; chairs with shiny wooden arms from the 1960s, nylon stretch covers and brocade cushions, a dining-table with plastic wood, place-mats with vintage cars on them.

But one thing is constant in all the houses: the warmth of the welcome. Here, you are always reminded that if the poor can be seen as victims, the working class are not. They may be under assault by those who are supposed to govern us, their confidence may be undermined by capitalist ideology, they may be treated with hostility or indifference by the media, but there remains a vast reservoir of resilience, decency and goodness. Not only this, there is an immeasurable quantity of unfulfilled talent, locked-up resources, unwanted energy and power that are only waiting for a moment of release, some energizing agent to express themselves. I am struck again and again by the intelligence which the society has no use for, the abilities that remain undeveloped, the talents that are not required by the marketplace. There is such an ugly and glaring mismatch between human needs and what money can buy. The comfort of people's homes, in contrast with the bleakness of the public areas, is a measure of the inturned nature of working-class culture and energy. But those things haven't gone away. They are only dormant. Because of the material changes of the last 25 years or so, it isn't easy to appreciate what a repressive time we have lived through, what a rejection of working-class creativity and what a stifling of ability.

Ron Pritchard is 58. He has whitening hair, bright eyes, but is thin and weakened by rheumatic fever and a double hernia. He lives in one room of his house, which is crowded and chaotic; a leatherette three-piece, a freezer, with teapot, cornflakes and milk on top, a bed with a multicoloured coverlet; a black plastic dustbin, a crate of lemonade bottles.

Ron's wife died a year ago. He doesn't want to go and live with his children, because he doesn't want to be pampered. His second great loss was giving up his selection of wild birds. His brother-in-law was prosecuted and fined £800 last year; so Ron reluctantly parted with his British song-birds and took to pigeons.

The loss was the more grievous because he has not been without birds since he was eight or nine. He says, 'I'm a British-bird man'; and in that phrase there is a passion for the countryside and its life and an understanding without equal in the West Midlands. 'I wouldn't give you 10 pence for a hundred canaries. The only birds I know are English wild birds. I love them. The law is stupid. But I will say this – the only people who should be allowed to keep them are those who care for them. Those who go out catching them just to make money, using bird-lime, they should be given a life sentence.'

He was feeling a bit low that Friday evening; but as he starts talking about his passion, he is newly animated; in spite of the sickness and the sadness of being alone, there runs through him something vibrant and living, a love of England that has nothing to do with the patriotism appropriated by those who own it.

Ron has been a polisher; one of those occupations with a high incidence of disease. And Ron looks older than his 58 years. But, as he speaks, he cups his hand, holding imaginary linnets or goldfinches, and he blows to ruffle the feathers in order to see whether they are in perfect condition, to tell whether they have been fed the right seed, to determine precisely what species they are.

'The secret of keeping wild birds is to feed them as they are fed in nature, not just giving them the same seed all the year round. You watch what they eat – for instance, in August the goldfinches feed on the 'sugar-babbies' [the seeds of thistles] as they blow all over the motorways and railway sidings. Then they'll go on to the 'hard-heads' when winter is coming up, the round seed they call niga. Then in the spring, when they're coming into condition for breeding, they'll feed off the dandelions. That's when they come into full colour, they lose the white spots off the wings.

'You have to know where they live in the wild and look after them accordingly. You'll find the bullfinch on the dock leaves when they go brown, linnets on wormwood in the spinneys, redpolls on the cats'-tails – that's willow. You watch them change colour with the season, see them go grey as sparrows this time of the year. Now, November time, you take a goldfinch, its beak is white with a black line; but when it's coming into condition, it'll lose the black and its beak'll go a pale pink, so clear it's like looking through glass.

'You have to colour-feed them in captivity. You see, they colour-feed themselves and so you have to do the same it they're to remain in the natural state. I give then red pepper before they moult. Otherwise, they'll lose that brightness and go dull. People don't know how to look after them. For instance, I always give them a tub of soft rainwater to bath in, you mustn't use hard water. At one show, the judge said to me, "Do you clean them in butter?" you should be able to put them in a bath of water and they would come out completely dry; because if the feathers are healthy, the water just shakes off. I feed them linseed and niga; red rape is the best conditioning seed.

'The close season is March and April, when they're nesting. Then they start getting more fierce. The best birds are May birds. They're in the peak of condition then. You have to make sure they're treated according to the season. They have to rough it, you must bring them down in the winter, then bring them back up in the spring. The late summer is the time for showing. I've only got to look at a bird; the bird itself tells you what condition it's in if you know anything about them.

'You catch them in a trap-cage. That doesn't hurt them. It's like three cages in one; the middle one is closed and that contains the decoy bird. The end ones have a trapdoor on top, with a spoon full of seed. You just leave it out in the field, the spinney, the garden. The bird comes down on to the seed, and the trapdoor opens and sends it into the cage.

'I've been out in the middle of winter, when the snow was deep on the ground; you push the snow out of the road with your boot, expose a patch of grass. Get a net, spread it on the grass. Then you get a bottle – hang on a minute.' He fetches a dark green bottle and a cork; he rubs the cork along the side of the bottle; it sounds just like a chirruping of linnets. 'You can see the linnets foraging for food in the snow, all balled up, with their feathers fluffed up, just as if they're going to die. So you set the net, spit on the bottle, rub it . . . All the birds come swooping down together. You could catch ten or fifteen at a time. You can take two or three of the best, let the others go.

'There's some hard men love birds. I've seen 'em fight rough, without a thought for hurting themselves or other people; but I've seen them break down and cry over a wounded bird. My love of British birds comes from my grandfather. My father wasn't interested, but my uncle used to take me out when I was a kid, catching finches. I'm against bulk catching. I'm against catching on lime. Birds ought to be only in the hands of those who know how to handle them. Some buggers might go out and catch two dozen; and twenty of them will die. They're only doing it for the money – because there is money in it. I'd give 'em bleeding life, I would.

'We had this ornithologist, he came to the club to give a lecture, with slides. Top man he was. He said you couldn't tell a cock from a hen of the mealy redpoll. I said, "Excuse me, you can." He said, "How?" Well, I knew that breed of redpoll, the cock carries a faint red speck each side of the head. I was right. He was the expert, he'd studied it for years, but he didn't know. What you know about birds, you know from handling them every day of your life, living with them.

'I'd got one goldfinch, I swore I'd never part with it. I'd had it for six or seven years and it was the best bird I'd ever had. When my brother-in-law got done, I thought, I ain't gonna get in no bother, I'll have to get rid of it. So I said to my mate, "Take me last bird." He says, "What shall I give you for it?" I said, "Nothing. Take it." So he takes it. A few days later, he says to me, "It's not as good as the one you gave me a couple of years ago." "I know it is. It's the best bird you'll ever have." He says, "No." "All right." He rings me up the next week. He says, "Listen to this." He's got the bloody phone downs the shed at the bottom of the garden and there's this goldfinch singing its head off over the phone. He says, "You were right. It's the one I fetched from your house." I said, "Ah, I know it is."

'Only cocks sing you know. There's nothing better in life that I know of than being out over the fields, the dead railways, the woods. It's illegal, of course. But then, the police have bought birds off me more than once. It's a joy, just to watch the birds change colour with the season; all your greys, end of August they're the colour of sparrows. The goldfinches now, end October, they'll have the heads red but the blaze will be dull. If I was to lose track of time, I'd know what time of the year it was just by looking at the birds.

'Since I had to give up the songbirds – oh, I do miss them. I've got pigeons now. I like them, but it isn't the same. I'll tell you something I've never told anybody before. You know the law says that all birds have got to be close-rung – that is, they ring them soon after hatching, to prove that they're aviary bred, and haven't been caught in the wild; so that they can be identified. Well, you're not supposed to be able to ring wild birds. A chap I knew, he smuggled three goldfinches in from Italy. They were beautiful. Two of them died, so there was just this one. There was only me could put a close-ring on a fresh-caught bird. You see, if a bird is kept in an aviary, it soon gets hard feet, like corns, through being on perches all the time. But a bird in the wild, flying around and settling on supple twigs and branches, its feet stay soft, no matter what age it is.

'Well, you cut the claws, very gently, being careful to avoid the vein. Then swill the foot under the tap. Then I put the foot in my mouth and hold it there for a long time; suck and suck and it goes like your fingers do after they've been in the bath for a long while, white and pliable. Then you can slip the ring over the three front claws, taking care to bend the back one properly so it slips over than too. Then you swill the foot under the tap again and it's done. Put it back in the flight. Then nobody knows it hasn't been aviary-bred. There aren't many people who know how to do that.

'When my brother-in-law got done, he was fined £800. Getting rid of my birds, it was like having my right arm off. But there's no sense in carrying on. If somebody has a grudge against you, they'll tell on you and it'll end up in court. And I'm the kind of person, if I can't have the best, I won't have anything.

'If I could have my life over again, I'd do the same thing. I was always brought up not to believe anything I was told and only to believe half of what I see . . . We were brought up hard; that's why the birds meant so much to us. They were instead of our freedom.'

The love of birds has been a long tradition in the West Midlands; the birds weren't only the obvious symbols of freedom, but they also legitimated tenderness and softness in a world that was often hard, even brutal. In Ron Pritchard, with his vast and detailed practical knowledge, it is a remembrance of a pre-industrial world, a defiance of the indignities of work, something wise and deep and passionate; part of the lasting defensiveness of the working class against poverty and humiliation; something proud and tenacious, the purest kind of love that acknowledges our kinship with all living things.

Perhaps the most common form of bird-keeping is the maintenance of a few pigeons in a shed at the bottom of the garden. Oliver Noakes is a few years younger than Ron and lives in an adjacent street. He has been a slaughterman, labourer and engineer. The last five years of his working life have been spent in an open-cast mine. Small but tough, he has reddish hair, a muscular body. He worked with a shovel, loading up the trucks with coal that was to be carried from the pit. He has a photograph of himself at work which he keeps in a brown envelope — a bulldozer and a crane, great yellow machines in a muddy pit, with layers of coal clearly visible around the sides; Oliver and his shovel are dwarfed by the machinery and the great excavation in the ground, perhaps 40 feet deep and 50 yards in diameter. Oliver says he has never been happier at work than when he was doing the heavy labour of shovelling. He enjoyed the rhythm, the exertion, the time it left him to think about things; the breaks, the comradeliness, the jokes. He has now been out of work for eight months and it is beginning to tell on him.

'We were brought up to work. You can't expect just to give it up and feel you're a free man. I know one thing. If you didn't think too kindly of people who were out of work before it happens to you, you soon change your opinion.

'I used to be so that I couldn't get home fast enough to do my pigeons. But when you've nothing else, you don't have the same the heart for it. I've had pigeons since I was five years old. They've been my life. I used to rush home from work and be down the flight even before I had my tea.'

Oliver is in five clubs; but he will have to give up membership of three of them, because membership costs £15 or £20 a year. On the sideboard are his trophies: silver, mounted on wood, a shield or a plaque. One is a graceful plinth with a silver-gilt pigeon on top; inscribed 'Saintes 1983'. Saintes is in Spain and that is the longest pigeon race of all – 475 miles.

While Oliver was working, he brought home £110-115 a week; and that was enough for the maintenance of the pigeons, the subscriptions, as well as the special feed, the tonic and conditioners racing pigeons need.

'When they fly back from Spain, it takes them about three days. They'll lose half their body weight on the flight. I feed them this tonic. The wife thinks I give them too much; when we used to take them down the club, people used to say, "Hey-up, here come the bloody ducks," they were that fat. But when mine came home, they were still pretty sleek, while all the others were skin and bone. Look, there's my pen.' He takes a big flash-lamp, opens the kitchen window; about 10 yards from the house are the lofts, built by himself, fine-mesh wire pen with a more substantial roost for night-time. There is a painted sign on the front of the structure, 'Ponderosa Lofts'. On the roof a white wooden balustrade to discourage the birds from landing on the roof when they arrive after a race. The birds have to fly straight into the loft, because, until they do so, you can't remove the rubber ring from their leg and clock them in.

'The first pigeons I ever had were when I was five. I went to Birmingham with my mam and dad and in the pet store I saw these beautiful fantails. I knew I wanted them. In fact I showed off so much, they bought them for me. I'm a bit upset today. I've had to have some of them killed off. They're getting old. I couldn't do it myself. I had to get a mate of mine to do it for me. You get so attached to them. When there's been anything wrong with them, I've been out there till two or three o'clock in the morning.

'You can start to race pigeons when they're as young as 11 weeks, from the Channel Islands; 16 weeks from Rennes and

Nancy; for the Spanish run you wait till they're a little older. They'll go through three or four seasons as a rule. I know all my pigeons, all 70 of them. I give a lot of them names. I had one called Walter, he was a beauty. He was on the Spanish run – you know how it works, do you? The container lorry comes and takes them all over there, then they are all released at a certain time. Anyway, I was expecting Walter to win. I had a phone call from a woman in Coventry. She had found Walter, he'd landed in her garden. I said to her, "Knock him up, will you." I meant scare him off, shoo him away with a towel or something. She thought I said, "Lock him up." When I rang up a bit later to see what had happend to him, she said she'd still got him safely at home. So I said, "No, no, let him go." And he still came in sixth! I thought, oh well, that won't happen again. Next time, he went to her again.

'Three days it takes from Saintes. When they fly over the water, of course they fly low, close to the sea. If a big wave comes, it can easily overpower them, it drowns them. Nobody knows how they do it, how they return from so far.

'I've had lots of prizes in my time. I'm happy with the trophies and the few quid you get. Of course, now, there's big money in it. Like everything else, all the working people's sports, they get turned into big business. I know one chap, he's won two or three thousand pounds this season. But you see then, you get people who don't do it for the love of the birds, they do it for money. If the bird doesn't win first time, they kill it and get a new one; and that's how they carry on until they do get a winner. I think that's wrong. I talk to mine, I call them when I go out. I speak to them all the time, "Come on, my beauties, come on, my babbies." The bloke next door, I think he thought I must be a bit simple. They threatened to set fire to the pen. I said, "You do, and you'll not bleeding walk away from it." He's in the nick now. Thieving.

'I wouldn't mistreat the birds. I wouldn't go in for what they call widowhood flying, I only do natural flying. Widowhood means that they keep the cock and hen birds separate. Natural means that they stay together all the time. With widowhood, what they do, they get a perspex screen, and keep the hen bird behind it, so the cock can see her but not get at her. He gets all excited, then you let them together just for a few seconds, not long enough for him to tread her. Then you take him out of the pen. Next day he goes racing; naturally, he flies home like a bat out of hell to get to her. When he gets back, he's shown her again, but they're not allowed to mate. That will happen every Friday through the racing season, April to October. Then one day a year, Boxing Day, he's allowed to tread her. You get an egg, but take it away from her before it's dry.'

Alice, Oliver's wife, comes in as he is speaking. She says, 'I think that's horrible. I wouldn't let him do that.'

'I wouldn't do it anyway.'

'The wives, they should do the same thing to their blokes if they do that. Let them find out what it feels like. No, go on, wait till Boxing Day. You can imagine what'd happen.'

'The young 'uns don't have the same feeling for the birds we have. They just want to win, they don't have the patience. There's a lad down this road, nice lad, but he's got rid of all his at the end of the season, because he can't be bothered with them all through the winter.

'This is the one sport where you still can't cheat. You have a clock, then when the bird comes back – all the clocks are set at the same time – you take the rubber ring off their leg, put it in a little container, slip it through the aperture on the clock; that punctures a card and records the time of arrival. Then you take your clock down to the clubroom. The clock is locked, so you can't open it. Well, you can unscrew the back, but you can tell if the screws have been tampered with. It has been known – they've re-set the mechanism, so it looks as if your bird has come home five minutes before anybody else's. The secretary of one of the clubs did it; his birds were always coming in just a few minutes ahead of everybody else's. One day, he hadn't rescrewed the back of his clock tight enough. They got him. And once you've been caught cheating in this sport, that's it. You're barred for life then. *Sine die*. Sigh and die, we call it. You'll never be allowed to compete again. It's nice to know there is at least one sport where you have to be honest.'

A black cat is sleeping in front of the fire. I said I always thought a cat among the pigeons was asking for trouble. 'No, well, we had him when our son was sick. We nearly lost him. Addison's disease.

And that was the one thing he wanted. But that cat has never been out the back. Never.'

Alice says, 'There's one thing. If your husband is a pigeon man, you always know where he is. I get as involved in it as he does.'

Five minutes away from where Oliver lives are the old people's flats. Mr Ager has just moved into a ground floor flat, because he can no longer climb stairs. He is a former miner, now 69. All old people who live alone in Walsall have been equipped with the Piper system: there is a cord, which, when pulled, causes a light to flash in an office in the civic centre, and there is immediately contact with whoever is on duty there. There is a cord in the bedroom, the kitchen and the hall and it reaches to the floor, so that even if an old person has fallen over he or she can still reach the communication system. Once contact is made, and the duty officer in the civic centre finds out what the trouble is, he or she telephones someone in the neighbourhood – there is a rota of volunteers – who will immediately go round to the flat, sort out the problem, fetch the ambulance, doctor or police. When the Piper system was first installed in the old people's flats, the idea was ridiculed by the local press and the opposition called it an unwarrantable extravagance, a waste of ratepayers' money. That isn't how the old people feel, those who live alone – they are reassured by the ready contact with the outside world; most say they know at least one person whose life has been saved by it.

Mr Ager started work when he was 13. He is one of those monumental working-class figures; silver-haired, well built, but grown stiff now with age. The afternoon we called on him, he was having a nap; and he came to the door full of sleep and slightly disorientated by the unexpected call. But he invited us in; and, as though it was the most expected thing in the world, began to talk about his life. He was one of 11 children. His mother died when he was six, leaving three children younger than he; she was worn out with work and childbearing at the age of 47. 'We slept four in a bed, top to toe. It was nothing to wake up in the middle of the night with somebody's foot in your mouth.

'There were six of us brothers, all worked at the same pit; and I joined them after my thirteenth birthday. When we were late, it was half the shift missing. We'd rush to the pit cage, just as they were taking the gates off it to make ready to bring up the coal. I wouldn't like to say how many years we gave to the pit between us. But even though I had six brothers with me, six blood brothers, I'd say I had more than that. Everybody was brothers down the pit. It united you, knitted you together. You made things easier for one another. If somebody was a bit slower, everybody would give him a hand, help him out.

'I remember there'd be men queuing up at the pit for a job every day. The manager would say to them, "Wait about a bit, there'll be somebody up in a minute." At the time, they had some new machinery, cutting machinery and nearly every day somebody got hurt. Sometimes, the bloke they brought up was in a sack, cut to bits. Then they'd say to whoever was waiting for a job, "All right, you can go down now."

'Accidents happened all the time. Twice I've been buried. Once I broke both my legs. And the ambulance had hard tyres, bumping on the road; getting to the hospital was an agony. One day I felt a rock fall on my foot. I thought nothing of it. Later on, my toe felt a bit sore and damp. I took my boot off and my toe had almost been severed. It was covered with blood. I never even had a day off for that. They talk about human life being cheap in India, China; it's been bloody cheap here, the history of labour in this country.

'When I first started, the pit where we were, you used to go down with tallow candles, had to hang your snap on some shot wire – you know, what they used for blasting – so the mice couldn't get at it. The mice used to come down in the corn they fed to the horses and the pit was swarming with them. Even then, I've seen the bloody mice climb up this shot wire, bite through the paper to get at your food. I'd always throw mine away if that happened; but you got damn hungry, some would just eat what the mice had left them.

'When I first started, I was paid 10 pence a day and you were paid by the bloke you worked for, sort of sub-contracting. Five shillings was my first week's wage. The bloke who owned the pit, you never saw him. He had agents and managers to do the dirty work for him.

'They had their money's worth out of us, 50 times over. And even though most of the pits where I worked at Cannock, they're closed now, but the poor buggers who worked in them still bear the scars. A pit closes, a factory shuts down, but that's not the end of it for the people. One chap I know, he'd been trying to get compensation for silicosis; seven years he'd been sent from one doctor to another. They wouldn't give him a penny, not until this had been checked and that had been verified. Seven years. In the end, he was awarded £7,000. He died the following week.

'When I was 32, I had miners' nystagmus. I had to come out of the pit. No work here, I had to go to Slough, in a factory, living in digs. My wife died at 47, the same age as my mother had been. I had to go back down the pit, nystagmus or no. I've worked in places where the roads were only two or three feet high; and you had to walk anything up to three miles before you started work.

'I am bitter, in a way. We expected so much better than what turned out. What have we got now – mass unemployment, poverty, war, who knows? We thought all these were things of the past; and here they are, facing us all over again. We were conned, make no mistake. We were told that we were going to make a new world, where all these could never happen again. So we agreed to make the system work. And then they try to turn it against us, the co-operation. It's our fault because the system doesn't work. They blame the working class, same as they always have done. It's their contempt for us that's hard to put up with. They might get away with it, for a time. But there's thousands learning, every day – every redundancy, every factory that closes, somebody is learning all over again the same hard truths that we did all those years ago.'

On the green in the very centre of the estate lives Jeff Watts; now in his thirties, four children. A wellbuilt and powerful man; a warm smile, full of energy. As he sits cuddling his youngest child in the late evening in front of the fire, it is difficult to imagine that he was, in his words, 'a right villain' when he was younger, 'always fighting'. Out of work for nearly three years, during that time he has trained four football teams from lads around the estate, the first of which is now third in the Midland Combination League. He organized some of the unemployed youngsters to help clear a piece of ground for the pitch, and help construct the stands, the changing rooms. He is proud that none of them asked for payment; all of it was done voluntarily; they worked for the pleasure of building something that was going to serve the neighbourhood. Jeff knows that what the youngsters need is something that will call forth their creativity and positive feelings. It's because nothing is ever asked of them that so many become destructive and violent. The football pitch and the amenities have never been vandalized. 'It belongs to them.' The first team are called the Kestrels; Jeff was out one day in the fields and saw a bird fly up which, he was told, was a kestrel. Kestrels are not common in that part of the country; so it seemed an appropriate name for the team. He is delighted with what he has achieved; he has used his time out of work positively. He is sick of hearing working people put down all the time. 'They try to tell us the unemployed are feckless, but there's some fantastic lads among them; boys with real skill who, if they had the chance, could do anything. They may not be clever with words, but all the skilled craftsmen we've always produced, they've still got it in them, only nobody wants to know.'

Jeff was one of a family of eight. When he was younger, he had the reputation of being a really hard man. His mate says, 'I've seen somebody hit him with a car jack, knocked him over; but he's got up and slugged them.' Jeff's family were a tough lot, with a terrible temper. They used to come from all over town to fight his brother, who was said to be unbeatable.

Jeff no longer has to show how tough he is. In any case, he has been softened by experience. 'You don't understand when you're young. For one thing, you don't realize what your parents do for you – all the things you take for granted. We were always fed and clothed, but when your mate had half a crown in his pocket, you resented it and thought, well, why couldn't my mum and dad give me half a crown as well? It's only later that you learn they did what they could for you and you'll never know what they had to go without themselves so that you shouldn't want for anything.' Jeff's daughter has leukaemia. She is 14. She has had blood transfusions and seems to be responding to treatment; and Jeff has been deeply touched by her dignity and courage. 'She's been marvellous. She has had to have this radiation treatment, where her hair falls out; but the way she's taken it is a lesson to anybody. She stays with her nan in between her spells in hospital, because she's very prone to infection and with the other kids there's always something going round. When the doctor told her what she was suffering from, she came out smiling. She said she was relieved to know what it was. She's been treated wonderfully by the staff at the hospital. Only there's a lot of equipment that the hospital ought to have but doesn't. We're doing a charity match to help raise some money towards a machine which analyses the blood and which costs half a million. We shan't make that much, but we'll do what we can. One of the lads made a good suggestion the other day. He said, "Instead of having collection boxes to help the hospitals, they should have boxes for voluntary contributions to cruise missiles; let the health service have the investment it needs, pay for bloody nuclear weapons by public subscription." You'd soon see a turn-around then. We're supposed to have a general election where all these issues were to have been discussed. Were they hell. You never heard any talk about dual-key, there was no real discussion. It's only now the election's safely out of the way that the real picture comes out. Reagan can set the things off it he wants to, put two fingers up to Thatcher. There's 102 American bases in this country. That makes us occupied, by my reckoning. How can all these weapons have anything to do with defence? They're about destruction. How many times over do you have to be able to destroy the world before you're safe?'

Richard Greaves is 73; another of those who started work at 13 in the pit. He was one of a family of 13. His father had inherited a farm but drank it all away and came to work in the pits as a horse-fettler. Dick left the pit during the miners' strike that followed the General Strike of 1926; but by 1931 he was unemployed. At that time there were still two other brothers and two sisters living at home with their mother and father. Only one sister was working. She had a job as a teacher. She was supposed to keep all seven of them on her salary.

'They stopped my labour money because there was one person

working in the house. It made a lot of families split up, because people got bitter and resentful, having to keep their grown-up brothers and sisters as well as their parents out of one wage. I had a friend, and he went to the Guardians to ask for a bit more money because his wife had had a babby. He was told he shouldn't have no more little bastards if he couldn't keep them.

'Well, there was nothing doing in Walsall, being unemployed. You just felt you were being a drain on everybody. Me and my mate decided we'd go on our push-bikes to look round the country, see if we couldn't find something. I told my mother, I said, "I'm going with Tommy Hodges, looking for work." "Oh, ah. When you coming back?" "I don't know. Expect me when you see me." You never said much, but you felt all choked up inside. So we went off on our bikes. July 1931. We were away a year. I had half a crown in my pocket, Tommy had ten bob in his. The day I went, I was courting, I'd promised to meet my girl that night. I never turned up. I often wondered what she thought.

'We went to Manchester, Liverpool, Newcastle. We biked all round the country, stopped off in all the little towns. There was no work anywhere. We found odd jobs. We'd go to a farm in the evening, tell them we were looking for work and had nowhere to sleep and could they let us have their barn for the night and in return we'd do any odd jobs that wanted doing. Nine times out of 10 they said yes. You'd get to sleep in the straw and a good breakfast for doing a bit of work – potato picking, fruit picking, seeing to the animals, mucking out yards, anything they wanted. When we had nowhere to sleep, we had to make do under the hedges. I didn't mind it. I always kept myself clean. I had a razor with me, managed to shave. Next morning you'd be off again, unless there was work that lasted maybe a few days. It didn't worry me.

'We had some good times as well. New Brighton, Wallasey.'

Dick fetches out a small sketch pad; on each page there is a pencil or crayon portrait of some of the girls he met on his travels in 1931; some of the pages are a bit yellow and curled up; some of the pencil markings have faded. But the pictures are all sensitively rendered and evocative of the time – girls in cloche hats, with marcelled hair, rouged cheeks; some smiling, some serious, some haughty, some beautiful, some plain. 'I'd draw their picture on the tram, on the beach, then show it to them. It was a good way of getting to know a girl. We didn't sleep in a barn every night, you know.' He smiles.

'It was a year later when I got back to Walsall. I shall always remember the day I came back. I was cycling down Bradford Street and I saw this girl being rough-handled by a man, being pulled about. I got off my bike. I said to her, "Is this man annoying you?" She said he was; so I offered to walk her home. She became my wife. We've been married 50 years.

'I've worked everywhere. I worked in a steel-rolling mill, polishing, labouring, anything. I didn't finish till three years ago. I was working in a pub till I was 70, cleaning. I wouldn't have left then, only the landlord's wife turned snooty with me over something and she told me off; then she said, "Oh, it's all right, I'm not dismissing you." I said, "No, you've no need to, I'm going of my own accord." I bet there isn't anybody in this country worked harder than I have. At the steel mill, I've gone to work at seven on Monday morning and not finished till nine the Tuesday night. Then I've worked Wednesday, seven till nine, Thursday seven till nine, then I've gone in Friday morning at seven till Saturday dinner-time one o'clock. The only breaks I've had, I'd cycle home for a meal, then straight back to work.

'I only took up painting and drawing again when I retired three years ago. I'd always done it as a kid, until I was 18. But after that, – apart from the sketches when I was away I didn't touch it for 50 years. But now I have taken it up again. These are some of my drawings.' He fetches some folders and larger sketch pads from the back room and spreads his work out over the chairs, table and the floor. Many of the drawings are of buildings, all executed with meticulous accuracy; some of them so fine they are like architect's plans: the old Guildhall in Walsall, the half-timbered houses in Droitwich, Hereford and Shrewsbury, canal and village scenes; each detail rendered even to the cracks in the stone and the irregularities of the medieval structure. He has a folder of faces, mostly in crayon, some in watercolours – chiefly portraits of celebrities – John Wayne and Charles and Diana; then a series of a Red Indian, a cowboy, a cavalier, a pirate. There are some pictures of his wife which he has taken from old and yellowing photographs, in which he has made her live again with the vibrancy and energy of her youth. There are some drawings of London – Buckingham Palace, St Paul's, London Bridge – taken from a series of old photographs. Dick Greaves is one of those many working-class people whose talents have not been used by the society. What place was there for an artist in Walsall in 1926, in lives darkened by poverty and industrial strife. All these abilities and powers had to be suppressed, made to languish and remain uncultivated.

This makes the re-emergence of his talent in his seventies all the more poignant. To the question of what might have happened if his ability had been recognised earlier, he answers without rancour, 'You can't say, can you? You can't say how your life might have been. No one saw what I could do; well, they did, I had my pictures shown in the town hall when I was at school. But those were thought of as childish pursuits if you came from the working class. Nothing was done to encourage them. They had nothing to do with the business of making a living. But if I had developed them, well, I might easily have never met my wife and I might have missed all the happy years I've had with her. And how are you to judge what kind of a loss that might have been? You can't set one thing against another like that.'

Mr Greaves has had an exhibition of his work in the Neighbourhood Office. There is little doubt that if his talent had been properly nurtured, he could have become a considerable artist.

In the atmosphere of defeat of the 1980s, it is easy to underestimate working-class people. Even the poorest, those who are bearing the brunt of the recession, can sometimes surprise you by their responses.

Pauline is 22; slight, with dark hair and eyes, she is a shy, rather nervous girl. She's just had twins, three months premature: one weighed only three pounds, the other two pounds fourteen onces. 'The water broke, and they took me into hospital. They gave me an injection to stop the labour; but they were born by Caesarean two days later.' It was just 25 weeks after conception. 'They were so small, I didn't dare pick them up. I try to go to see them every day at the hospital, but it costs me 80 pence return on the bus, and 20 pence for the other children – that's Jackie, five and Jason, four. I'm only getting £32 a week, and £11.70 child allowance.'

Pauline left her husband after years of quarrelling. He first of all tried to control her by verbal bullying and then by hitting her. She left home with the two children one night, after he had hit her with a monkey-wrench. It was two o'clock in the morning. 'I just took the kids and got out. I went to my husband's sister at first and then later to my own sister in Wolverhampton.' She was eventually allocated a flat and moved in with the two children, who were then still babies. There was no gas, no electricity or heating in the flat. She dragged a bed off the tip on the edge of the estate and raised it on some bricks. The promised visit from the DHSS took several weeks.

Pauline left school at 16; and was married on the following Saturday. At 22, she has four children. She has difficulty with reading and writing. She is a sensitive and intelligent girl, devoted to her children and determined to bring them up well.

'I went home one night, and there were six policemen waiting outside my door. Somebody had told them I was mistreating the children. I'd been round my friend's for the evening, I was carrying Jason in my arms, Jackie was walking. It was late – it was half past ten, but I'd rather take the children with me than leave anyone else with them. The police said I'd been beating them. I said, "You can take them and examine them if you like." They said that was what they were going to do anyway. So they took us, there and then, down to the police station. They kept us there till two o'clock in the cowing morning. There was a bruise on Jason's leg where he fell down; nothing else. I said, "I've never mistreated my kids, but I call this mistreatment, being kept here till two in the morning."

'I'm not very happy about living here; but I've good friends. I don't know what I would have done without them. It was terrible when I first moved in here. There was a murder three doors away. I saw them take the body out. Her husband had found her with another bloke and had just smashed her face in. I felt funny about living here after that happened.'

Pauline's looks like an unhappy story at first sight. But she has great courage and is resolved not to be defeated. She is learning to battle for her kids, to get what she is entitled to from the DHSS; she is practising her reading and writing; goes to the Neighbourhood Office for help with budgeting. But perhaps the most touching moment was when she took out the books she has filled with her drawings: sketches of birds, horses, ornaments, faces; familiar objects, all carried out with great delicacy and skill; all completely spontaneous; the resolution of a sensitive and indomitable spirit, trapped in circumstances by which she is determined not to be defeated.

It's impossible to avoid the evidence of all the energies and skills that have been suppressed in working-class people and then continue to be suppressed today. In the 1920s and 1930s, it was grinding poverty and hunger; in the 1980s it's the ceaseless onslaught of capitalist selling and advertising and money worship, its shadows and substanceless entertainments, all the trivial and thoughtless distractions and purchased consolations which are offered to people as a substitute for allowing their deepest powers and possibilities to flower and express themselves. And yet, if all the rejected attributes and capabilities were to find release, what a wealth of creativity and invention would be discovered. It lies merely fallow, not destroyed. So many of the cliches about 'self-realization' and 'developing the potential of the individual' are quite hollow in working-class experience, when the society is designed to do for them the very opposite. This is one of the long-term visions of those who have conceived the neighbourhood idea, that we have more in us than is ever demanded and that our human substance will not be content for ever to accept that alien evaluation of us by the rich and powerful that we are where we deserve to be. The regeneration of neighbourhood and community can be achieved only by what is in them; and that means the stifled diversity, richness and creativity of working people themselves.

5. The Walsall initiative

> We had this dream of what the Neighbourhood Offices should be like; an idea, a vision. But it's the kind of thing that if you've got to pass resolutions to achieve it, you'll never get anywhere. That's the biggest obstacle in local government. The officers say, 'Write down exactly what you want, and that will be done.' But it isn't the kind of thing that can be expressed like that. You can't write down what a dream is in a council resolution.'
> — Dave Church, housing chairman, 1980-82

In the 1960s, there was a considerable surge of community action, in response to the convulsions that were taking place in the centre of the big towns and cities, the grandiose 're-development' plans, the partnership between local authorities and private developers to build shopping complexes, expressways and car-parks, and large-scale slum clearance schemes. These plans often struck at settled working-class communities, many of them unsettling the old and the poor, many of these places were already in a state of disintegration through blight and substandard housing.

Much of the community action of this period was led by middle-class newcomers – young professionals, university students who had found cheap housing in the old working-class areas. The action groups were often extended campaigns and, although widely supported by the residents of any area, they didn't have the impetus of long-term mass involvement. People moved on; the immediate reason for the action disappeared – councils modified their plans, made concessions; areas were cleared, roads were constructed or the money ran out and they were postponed; people were re-housed on new estates. Action groups became institutionalized, the mass support of the early years fell away.

In Walsall it was different. The original inspiration of a community group later came to offer a rudimentary model of what was meant by neighbourhood. (This isn't to say that the Caldmore Residents' Action Group offered a blue-print: obviously the problems of a blighted inner-city area in 1970 are different from those of a neglected 1930s council estate in the 1980s.) At that time, Caldmore consisted of a series of traditional red-brick streets; there was a high proportion of immigrants, some of the people were owner-occupiers, others were renting from private landlords; a number of houses in the worst streets were owned by the council and used as temporary accommodation for homeless families and those with problems. It had always been a Conservative district.

At that time, Barrie Blower was in his twenties, living with his parents in one of these streets, and was trying to get the landlord to install a bathroom and inside lavatory. At the same time Brian Powell – later to become leader of the council – having just lost a safe Labour seat in another ward stood for Labour in Caldmore and received 400 votes against a Conservative vote of 2,000 or so. The third founder member of the Caldmore group was a young sociologist who had just come from Nottingham and was teaching at the Technical College.

When I first saw Caldmore in the early 1970s, it had all the familiar signs of neglect. Houses remained unoccupied for long periods and fell into disrepair: windows were broken, doors ripped off, children used them as playgrounds, people slept rough in them. Throughout the area were spaces where sites had been cleared, but rubble and waste remained on the open ground; to which garbage and discarded furniture were added, with the result that parts of the district were like a tip. The centre of the neighbourhood was Caldmore Green: a characteristic ninteenth-century industrial suburb: little dress shops with plaster models from the 1930s, an Indian grocery, a dingy Co-op with its green and white tiles, a shabby cinema, changing its programmes every day in an attempt to win back audiences, a cavernous Liberal Club and a Conservative Club.

The landlords of the houses – many of them old themselves – found they couldn't maintain their property; even some of the owner-occupiers found the expense of repairs beyond them; a husband died, an old woman went to live with her children, so that yet another house was left to the rats and the vandals. Younger people moved in by the council tended to be demoralized and in debt; those who had bought houses simply as a means of entering the housing market had little sense of involvement in the place. An increasing number of immigrants bought houses at inflated prices: having no experience of the housing market, they were being offered houses for £2,000 or more, when these had been changing hands at only a few hundred pounds. In the absence of any help to the newcomers or any attempt at political or social education of the people who had always lived in Caldmore, barriers of distrust and fear grew readily. The older people didn't understand. I remember one woman saying, 'I know we'm in the Black Country, but it never meant this.' People saw what had always prided itself on being a respectable area falling into rapid decay.

Barrie Blower, who had lived in Caldmore all his life, could feel the bitterness and isolation of people grow. 'My dad worked on the railways, and where we lived was quite close to the railway sheds and junction. My mum worked, metal polishing, because the pay on the railways was poor. There were five of us in the family. The house was on of a terrace and we shared toilets with the next-door neighbours and we had a communal yard. It was only half a mile from Walsall town centre and it only cost a halfpenny on the bus, but I never even saw Walsall town centre till I was seven. I didn't need to, because everything was here. There was the picture house, the shops, but especially the family and the neighbours. We were self-contained. It was a village within the town: a community. We all shared poverty; and if we weren't aware that it was poverty, it was because we shared something more significant and that was each other's lives. I knew not just the people in my street, but I knew a lot about all their lives – about 200 families. I can lie in bed at night even now and I still know all about them, what happened to them. We were reared by each other. I was taken in by the women three doors away when my mum was working and my mother took her kids in when she was sick. This isn't an argument for poverty; it's an argument for community. If anybody tells you that when you've got a bit more money you can dispense with other people – well, I shouldn't have thought it was something anybody needed to discuss.'

Barrie Blower went to grammar school, following what was to have been the familiar upward journey of so many bright working-class children in the early 1950s. He was expelled two years later, because – although he didn't realize it then – he resented the way in which he was being re-shaped in a way that separated him from his background. He left school at 15 and followed his father briefly into the railways, but soon left to join the navy. He was a stoker; but became the welfare representative on every ship he was on. 'I always had a sort of feeling for people. I wasn't clever and I didn't have any skills. But I always had this passion about people not being treated fairly.' Later, he became shop steward at the power station where he worked, in the steam and boiler-house. 'Working conditions were terrible. The ash-pits, there were these old men in their sixties, having to pull out red-hot clinker, the dust and the ash, inhaling it for years. They were dropping like flies. They called me a red: even though I knew nothing about politics. It was just a feeling of outrage that people should be treated like that; and it should just be accepted.

'Anyway, in 1970, the feeling was that Caldmore was a respectable, well-established sort of place going down in the world. It was a breeding ground for working-class reaction and nothing was being done about it. The Labour Party always had this laissez-faire reaction to social change. A lot of the old dears would look over the garden wall one day and see a woman with five kids, who, if she could have understood the language, would have recognized them to be in the same position that they'd been in themselves 40 years earlier. But they could only speak Gujarati. So although they didn't actually hate the neighbours, they hated the situation of having nobody to talk to. If they managed to persevere, they found, of course, that the values of the immigrants were the same as their own – hard work, family solidarity, neighbourliness. That was one of the great ironies; and it's one of the things we really worked on in the Caldmore Residents' Association. And this is one of those rather rare things now – a really successful integrated community.

'One story I think shows it quite well. There was a woman in our yard called Fanny Gilbert, the fat busybody type of person, the layer-out and pennies-on-the-eyes sort, solid and reliable. Anybody in trouble, giving birth – you'd fetch Fanny and out she'd come with her kettle – the universal working-class woman everybody knows about. She used to say to everybody, "I don't want these black 'uns round us. I can't understand them and I hate the smell of their cooking." One night a Gujarati knocked on my door in a panic. I didn't know what he wanted but it appeared his wife was about to give birth and they wanted me to phone for the ambulance. It was too late for that. So I thought, Fanny. So I just hammered on her door, and said, "Over the road." She'd been doing it so many years, she wasn't going to stop now. So out came the water, the towels, out came everything, the kettle; and she dashes across the street and delivers this kid. She had experienced something; and she learnt from it. It changed her, because her heart was stronger than the ideas she had.'

In September 1970, Brian Powell suggested that they should get some local people together to clear the land on a site where a child had been hurt. 'We leafleted the houses in the streets all round this place – a real dump it was was and we called a public meeting. The evening was pissing with rain, there was a John Wayne film on telly. I thought nobody would turn up. There was a massive turnout and we formed the Caldmore Residents' Association.

'Walsall council had never seen anything like it. We really unleashed some energy. A safe Tory seat as well. Nobody had given a thought to Caldmore for years. We gave an ultimatum to the council: if you don't clear the land by 30 October, we'll do it ourselves. We were told that we would be trespassing. Never mind, that's what we're going to do. The day arrived. The bailiffs came. The police came. We had hired a mechanical digger; we had an Irish bloke driving it. Bailiffs came and gave him a piece of paper to sign, saying that he'd received their warning. "Piss off." They went to get the police to nick him for refusing to sign. "I can't fucking write." The police could be seen to be acting against the whole community. They didn't like that. We had taken on the whole local authority; and they had to take notice. We fought through the media and they, of course, loved us. We said we would take over every house in Caldmore that was empty, do them up ourselves, do the repairs, refuse to pay rent and get squatters in every one. We were seen to be independent of the local authority. That's where the community groups have got to keep their independence, not to be sponsored by the local authority. We used to pay sixpence a week towards the Action Group fund. It's all theatre; but then, politics and religion, what else are they?

'The problems of Caldmore in 1970 are vastly different from those of Blakenall or Delves in 1983; but the principle is the same. Groups can be built around different issues – unemployment, poverty. It's harder to get people to unite in the poverty of the 1980s; people have learnt that individual survival is the answer and have lost the way into collective action. It's the tragedy of our times, the superstition of belief in money. The richest resource we have is each other; if we realize that, we can get all the material help we require and not sacrifice all the other things that get ridiculed, like relationships, neighbours, the life of the spirit.'

The Caldmore Advice Centre was set up in a disused shop on the Green; and this was the inspiration for the Neighbourhood Offices in the sense that no limit was set to the kind of issue that the centre was prepared to deal with. So many areas of our life have been labelled 'private' and removed from political debate, with the result that what passes for political discussion sounds thin and one-dimensional to those it concerns most closely. Caldmore – and later the Neighbourhood Offices – rejected this idea and tried to retrieve for public discussion precisely all those human things that have to do with living together, our relationships with each other – that 'unnatural environment of the private cell', Blower calls it.

Barrie Blower's involvement with the housing conditions of Caldmore eventually led to the formation of a housing association.

This started off on a small scale, building houses and flats on sites between demolished houses and pieces of spare land. But it has grown in scale and scope, with the result that the housing association has virtually transformed Caldmore and now owns something over 800 houses. And it is a very different transformation from any local authority house-building programme. It has been consistently low-rise, and on a human scale; not too high density and with accommodation for a wide variety of people — families, old people, single people, disabled. It forms a dramatic contrast with the tower blocks on the edge of Caldmore. It has faced and tried to resist those destructive tendencies that have been at work in so much redevelopment; and is as humane and responsive to the needs of the people as it is possible to be. Of course, Caldmore isn't going to offer a model for transcending society; and you hear the same complaints there as anywhere else. For instance, the first week I was there in 1983, there had been a falling away of numbers of old-age pensioners meeting in the Neighbourhood Office because of the spate of muggings that had occurred on the concrete car-park which separates the office from the main road.

In the early 1970s meanwhile, Brian Powell was working with the Caldmore Action Group, a process of political education that went in tandem with the fight for renewal of the area. This coincided with the unpopularity of the end of the Heath government, but, even so, in 1972, Powell was elected in Caldmore: Labour 1,900 votes, Conservative 1,700; the first time Labour had taken what had always been regarded as a seat not worth fighting.

Brian Powell had left school at 15 and was apprenticed to a printing firm. The company had a reputation for dismissing apprentices as soon they could command a full wage and taking on youngsters more cheaply. Powell was a good worker and was one of the few to be offered a permanent job when he'd served his apprenticeship. He told his employer, 'I'm going to do to you what what you've done to hundreds of others – I'm walking out of here on my twenty-first birthday.' He has always had an instinctive resentment of the way the poor are browbeaten. He has tried to organize in every place he has worked; and for this he was sacked seven times. He says it became an annual event for him to be chucked out for his political views. He has several times received the classic threat from employers that they would see to it he never gets another job in this town. He is a man of great energy and imagination; and is moved by his love of Walsall, a strong sense of commitment to place. Every time he goes away, he feels a sense of excitement in coming back; even though Walsall looks an undistinguished and far from attractive place, with its Victorian streets, its ill-defined boundary, its haphazard growth. Powell is affronted by the destructive influences that undermine our sense of belonging to a distinctive place – the ugly uniformity of shopping centres, the sameness of 'developers', the standardizing of 'dwelling units'. He is irreverent towards officials and professionals, sceptical of expertise, impatient of all the good sound reasons why nothing should be done to disturb the status quo; an enemy of custom and precedent.

The experience of Labour control in Walsall in the early seventies was an important learning experience for Powell as it was for Dave Church, who was chairman of housing when the Neighbourhood Offices were set up. Dave Church was from a completely non-political working-class family. Church was a metal worker, who happily accepted demotion to the warehouse so that he would be able to fit in his council work; and eventually he lost his job altogether, because he refused to neglect the job of setting up the Neighbourhood Offices; at the time of most intense activity, in early 1982, the offices were opening all over Walsall at the rate of two or three a week.

Many of the Labour group during 1973–76 had that experience that was common to so many Labour councillors up and down the country. They had come to join a council, in which Labour no longer seemed to ask questions, but merely accepted its role as part of the machinery; even though at this time it was quite obvious that the process of emotional detachment of large numbers of working people from commitment to Labour was growing. It was a period when many of the older councillors, perhaps exhausted by long years of service, tended to fall into the complacency of saying that they had done what they were put there to do, that it was just a question of tinkering with the nuts and bolts, that there were no more major causes to be fought for. The younger members felt that an opportunity was being lost, but weren't quite sure what they could do; they certainly didn't want to wait until they inherited senior positions in the structure and then simply administer a system that had grown not merely old, but also remote and inefficient. When Labour lost control, they formed what later was called the Tribune Group; and they met formally once a week, and informally all the time, in pubs, clubs, each other's houses, to talk about what ought to be done, to examine the limits and possibilities of local initiatives. Dave Church says, 'At this time I had the dream of co-operatives. I thought we could arrange it so that the whole of an estate would be completely free to run itself, nothing to do with the council. The idea of people determining their own needs and carrying out their own plans was already there. But we discussed everything under the sun. We had some wild and wonderful schemes; nothing was closed to discussion. And the Tribune Group gradually attracted more and more people. We gained ground in the Labour Party; and, after the election in 1980, we were able to defeat the old right-wing leadership. We were all working people, living locally. We didn't move in from outside, we didn't do it for reasons of left-wing dogma, we were just responding to the grumbles and complaints of the people we were supposed to be serving. You couldn't miss people's complaining – the council were too distant, they couldn't get their repairs done, to get a transfer was like getting out of Sing-Sing; the council was treated with at best indifference, often contempt and sometimes loathing. We felt that the previous period of Labour control had been no such thing; it might have been Labour, but control it wasn't. We wanted to make sure that we would do something purposeful to answer the kind of things people were actually saying. We didn't talk: we listened.'

It was during this period that the ideas of what could be done in practice within a period of office finally came to the concrete proposal of the Neighbourhood Offices. This was expressed in the manifesto, which was written within the pre-election period of 1980, *Haul to Democracy*. It wasn't a list of impossible demands; even less was it a catalogue of vague and well-meaning phrases –

the kind of staple local council election phamphlet, with a picture of the home-loving family man saying how much he cares about attracting industry and improving services to the community in which he is negotiating to buy a house. *Haul to Democracy* was an extended and reasoned account of what could be done; all of it legal, practicable, and quite capable of achievement within a period of Labour control. There was no attempt at concealment; it would cost a certain amount of money; new appointments would have to be made and these would be appointments of those who showed themselves to be aware of the problems facing working-class communities. *Haul to Democracy* was the result of that creative period in opposition that was fruitfully and capably used. When Labour took control in May 1980, the group knew they had to act quickly. The majority was only about eight. One thing that had been learnt from the earlier period was that councillors tend to spend the first two year learning how the system works, trying to find their way through the labyrinth of the bureaucracy, and the next two years looking over their shoulder at the electorate, trying not to say anything that will given offence to any group of voters.

They had also mastered council procedure to the last details. The first thing to be done was to set up the Reorganization Subcommittee, which was able to take to itself all the legal powers the council possessed. This committee could meet on a weekly basis, thereby shortening the usual committee cycle of six weeks. It meant that powers did not have to be dispersed in such a way that all the obstacles and doubts and sound reasons for not doing anything could delay the putting into practice of the manifesto's programme. The officers of the council were, of course, bound to co-operate with implementing council policy; but so many people had had experience, not of the ill will of the officers, but of the way in which the services tended to run along the grooves that already existed; slow, cumbersome and unpredictable; and the last thing they wanted was for the plan to be diminished or whittled away by bureaucratic modification or delay. When it first came to Neighbourhood Offices, the officials at first offered empty houses anywhere on the estate, up a cul-de-sac, off the main road, a hard-to-let house out of the way; with no particular relationship to the neighbourhoods at all. Dave Church thinks this was typical of lack of imagination; Brian Powell attributes it to obstructiveness.

It remained for the neighbourhoods to be defined; and that could only be done by consulting people from the different districts in town. Everyone recognizes the limits, the boundaries of his or her local area. They vary in size; some are quite small enclaves, like Goscote, with only a few hundred houses; others are much bigger estates. Nor was it difficult to locate the central point of the neighbourhood, where the office should be placed. Where possible, existing buildings – a library, a shop – could be converted; but for the most part, the offices were purpose-built and distinctive prefabricated buildings, painted black, with the Neighbourhood Office logo conspicuously displayed. As you go round Walsall, they are very easy to spot; in fact, it comes as something of a surprise to learn that there are only 31 of them. Originally, there were to have been 34; 33 opened before Labour lost control and two have been closed down by the 'anti-socialist coalition' (Conservatives, Liberals and Independents, who have governed the town since May 1982. It is actually not easy for Liberals to underwrite a policy of closing offices, with their much vaunted attachment to community politics.)

Of course mistakes were made. One of the most obvious was the failure to consult staff in the housing department before the scheme was put into practice. Dave Church imagined that the people administering the service would be so delighted to have their jobs upgraded and made more interesting that it didn't occur to them that there might be resistance.

Dave Church: 'Staff in the department had never been asked anything about anything; ever. People had been there for 10 years and had never spoken to the housing manager since the day they were appointed. A lot of them were doing jobs that were driving them round the twist – can you imagine, someone doing nothing for 20 years but letting garages, things like that. I though that because it would enrich their jobs, they would be all for it.

'I called two meetings of all the housing staff. I really ought to have remembered how I used to react when I worked in a factory if anybody tried to bypass the unions and go straight to the workforce. There was no excuse really, we were just carried away with enthusiasm; we thought everybody would feel the same. We put the idea to them; all right. The first question I was asked was whether I could guarantee that there would be no redundancies. Well, I thought we would be taking on staff. I knew the service was going to expand. But, in all honesty, I couldn't guarantee that not one job loss would occur somewhere. So I said I couldn't say that. I said you can see the manifesto — it means more jobs, and more money for a lot of people working in the department, much more job satisfaction. As it turned out, there weren't any redundancies; and I could have satisfied them by giving that guarantee. But we remembered how Labour administrations have failed to carry out their promises and I didn't want to fall back into those bland reassurances that were so typical of the old politics.

'In fact, the questions people asked slightly took me aback. We had this vision, we were coming here with this idea of transforming the system and people wanted to know how they would be compensated for loss of subsidized canteen meals when they were out in the Neighbourhood Offices; they wanted to know how they would get to work, if they were no longer commuting into the town centre. It's an interesting exercise, to see how easily the visions can get blocked by people's tendency to cling to the old familiar ways. You don't realize people's fear of change; the basic conservatism of British people.

'The upshot of it was that Nalgo blacked the first posts that were advertised. I should perhaps say that the first lot of advertisements that went in were drafted by the personnel department and they were very much the traditional local authority advertisements. We didn't appoint anyone from those, but re-shaped the advert, so that we should be sure of getting people who were committed, who knew something of what was expected in working-class communities, where the offices were to be a vital growing force in the place.

'Anyway, the people who were supposed to be giving out the application forms for the first posts refused to handle them. We made a big deal over it; was their immediate superior aware that they weren't doing the job asked of them? Yes. Was the deputy housing manager aware that this was going on? Yes. So we sacked all of them. Just like that. Naturally, that brought the whole housing department out. It was what we expected. We got the full-time official down from Nalgo that same afternoon and when we explained to him what the decentralization process actually involved, how obvious it was that it could bring nothing but benefit to his people, it was all sorted out. In fact, it was really an elementary failure in communication; we should have started off talking about the new jobs, the enhanced status, the increased satisfaction. The trouble was, we didn't have the negotiating method that was appropriate to the speed at which we were trying to work. We got an agreement to have the representatives from Nalgo and from the joint shop stewards from the manual unions on the Reorganization Subcommittee with us. That way, they could advise about the grading of new posts, what where the appropriate levels and so on. After that, we had no more disputes.'

Naturally, many of the staff were apprehensive about the changeover. In the fastness of the civic centre, many of them had had little or no contact with the people they were supposed to serve; personal contact – on such rare occasions as it had been unavoidable – had nearly always meant some more or less frightening confrontation with a tenant driven to despair by neglect and indifference and who had somehow managed to evade the elaborate defences provided by the civic centre. One elderly woman, who had worked in the housing department for 30 years, and who had fiercely resisted the change, found, to her delight, that it gave her an energy and involvement in her work which she had never thought possible: 'You come to think of the public as your enemy. Because you only ever hear from them when there's a complaint, you think of them as slightly less than human. You'll do anything to avoid them. The idea of being in a Neighbourhood Office, on show to the public, even visible behind a plate-glass window, it scared a lot of us.'

There had always been receptionists in the town hall who had dealt with queries. But all that had reached the upper storeys of the building were often half-truths and exaggerations of skirmishes that had occured when people, driven beyond endurance by the failure to get a repair carried out or a desperately needed rebate, had lost their temper. Success had never been visible, and, for the most part, even those people who were working away to make the system operate properly seldom received any acknowledgement of what they'd achieved. Most of the housing department were convinced and there was a good deal of commitment by the time the scheme began. Those who seemed dead set against it were distributed around the Neighbourhood Offices in such a way that they were surrounded by people who were enthusiastic in their commitment. The neighbourhood officers were told not to allow individuals to wreck things. And in the end, most people have adapted well. Dave Church says he knows of a few who were out-and-out racists and some of them are now staying behind in the evenings on a voluntary basis to help organize social events for old-age pensioners or black teenagers.

'You have a dream and you have to put it in the form of a council resolution. The structures, the whole style of the bureaucracy only trap dreams, destroy them. That was why the people we wanted to appoint as officers had to be able to have the sympathetic understanding of the issues in poor or working-class communities. That's why we had that phrase in the manifesto about "people akin to our philosophy". That was when the press really attacked us, accused us of creating jobs for the boys and all that. Of course, the rich and powerful appoint their supporters and henchmen all the time, and nobody dares raise a murmur; but you get someone who wants to help the powerless and the poor and you get accused of all kinds of malpractice. It's funny how the public interest always coincides with the interest of the people with power. We felt that we'd been elected to carry out this very ideal, this dream, and therefore we couldn't achieve it without people sympathetic to its realization. The press tried to create the idea that it was your mates and cronies, using ratepayers' money to help your friends. At one point, I got pushed by the press and when I was asked, 'Would you appoint a Conservative to the post of neighbourhood officer?' I said it was unlikely. But then it was unlikely that a Conservative would apply. It wasn't knocking anybody to say that. If I was appointing the managing director of British Nuclear Fuels, even if the guy sitting in front of me was the best physicist Cambridge could produce, I still wouldn't appoint him if he'd spent all his waking hours working for Friends of the Earth, would I? It's a pernicious myth that there is anything "non-political" about these things. "Non-political" invariably means supporting the existing state of affairs.

'This was our most difficult moment in the whole operation. Under this pressure from the media – and that was the purpose of the attack – the right in the Labour group lost their nerve; or maybe they saw their chance to recapture control of the group. But nearly half of them put down a notice of motion for the next council meeting. This was because they wanted to go back to the manifesto and redefine what we had meant when we said we were looking for people akin to our philosophy. They were afraid we would lose support. Some of them said we'd gone too far. But nobody had raised any objection when the manifesto was written or when we had fought the election.

'Needless to say, the press went to town on it: 10 brave councillors standing up for their consciences. So we had a crisis meeting of the Labour group and put down a resolution that the notice of motion should be withdrawn. The chief executive insisted that everyone should withdraw his or her name, or the notice of motion would still stand. In the end, they did all withdraw, even the man who initiated notice of motion; but then he resigned and left the party. It was a shame – he was a good party stalwart but, after he'd gone that far, he couldn't really climb down. So he felt he had to give up everything.'

Since 1982, there has been a sense of marking time. The threat from the opposition has been always present; there have been threats to close Neighbourhood Offices – not all of them, but especially in Conservative areas. In fact, two have been closed; and, even in one of these, a petition was circulated that gathered 3,000 signatures. It is a mistake to believe that only the working-class areas are the beneficiaries of the neighbourhood idea. Indeed, in one of the most prosperous parts of Walsall, a surprisingly high number of householders qualify for rate rebates; and they have not, on the whole, been slow to avail themselves of the opportunity.

The creative force that was only beginning to express itself in the setting up of the Neighbourhood Offices is far from spent. There has been some demoralization among staff – a few of the officers have moved on, taking their experience to what are regarded as safer Labour areas. The actual achievement in the neighbourhoods is variable. At the very least, in those places where little more than the administrative convenience of decentralization has been realized, the gains are conspicuous. But in other areas – as in Blakenall – there are real stirrings of people demanding change; while in Goscote, a transformation has occurred. In all offices, there has been a growing pressure on services. People have been given fresh confidence that they can work for their own neighbourhood to get things done – help the unemployed, get a community centre, petition over bus services or road saftey. Many of the myths of the council and its power have been dispelled. It isn't so intimidating. The people who staff the offices do not wrap themselves in a cloak of professional jargon and mystery. The limits of the council's power are visible; the cuts and limits imposed by central government become plainer.

The real innovation in Walsall has been the imagination and inventiveness that have been brought to politics; the fact that political discussion involves our whole lives, our relationships, our feelings for one another, is a living expression of our deepest hopes and fears; is something far more than the two-dimensional preoccupation with mere administrative convenience; and is something far richer and more complex than the cardboard cut-out of a working-class that figures in the rhetoric of the far left.

6. Media Responses

When you hear people talking about the horrors of the one-party state, they don't stop to think. We have a one-party state too – the capitalist party. People elect candidates for the political party, maybe Tory, maybe Labour, maybe Liberal. But they're all different tendencies in the capitalist party. That's why you hear people say, 'They're all the same.' Tweedledum and Tweedledee. One lot indistinguishable from another.
— Brian Powell, leader of the Walsall council, 1980–82

If there had been any doubt about the importance of the work being done in Walsall, the response of the media would soon reassure us. Sometimes, it seems, the reaction of the enemies of socialism is a truer guide towards real socialist initiatives than the sometimes half-hearted or even dismissive attitude of the left.

For a time Walsall had the distinction of being singled out as the embodiment of 'left-wing extremism'; that shifting role which is visited on various Labour-controlled authorities in turn, in order to terrify the nation that it is trembling under the constant threat of a red take-over, mini-Kremlins, the totalitarian menace that comes from the poor and uemployed of a depressed inner-city borough or nothern town. The GLC, Lambeth, South Yorkshire, Lothian and, for a time in 1980-81, Walsall, have all been the object of intemperate attack for their (mostly) rather modest attempts to use the cumbersome and rusting machinery of local administration for the benefit of the disadvantaged and unprivileged in their area. This is what has led to a tightening of control and punitive action by a central government, whose party has traditionally claimed to be the champion of local freedoms and initiatives. It is clear that the Conservative Party in the 1980s is, in many ways, the reverse of what its rhetoric has for so long proclaimed: it turns out to be a vigorous supporter of the concentration of power, the intensification of state control – which it pretends to abhor – over the lives of people; it goes along with those processes at work in the worldwide empire of capital, which diminish local power everywhere – the great concentrations of capital, the transnational corporations, the imposition of the uniform global tune of money to which we are all made to dance; ironically, even the power of the country to which they claim such an attachment is being curtailed, so that it is transformed into a mere offshore island in the great imperial capitalist project.

It is worth looking at what was said of the Walsall undertaking by the short-lived Labour administration from May 1980-82. The lasting testimony to the effectiveness of that administration is the fact that, even when Labour lost in 1982, the Neighbourhood Offices were already part of the landscape and could not be so readily abolished by the opposition.

Of the national press, the *Daily Mail* fearlessly rooted out the danger, only four months after Labour had come to power. 'This Little Kremlin at the Heart of England', its feature article was headed. The neighbourhood scheme is described as costing £2.3 million; including £500,000 on council house improvement and £100,000 on mobile neighbourhood housing and advice centres. "Crazy," snorts Independent councillor, Sid Wright . . . "We've already tried one of these mobile advice centres, a Range Rover with caravan, and it flopped" . . . Within three months, Walsall has been made a byword for doctrinaire Socialist excess and eccentricity . . . Since May, Walsall has been ruled by a party within a party – a cabal known as the Tribune group, whose 20 members and sympathisers happen to be chairmen and vice-chairmen of every important committee of the council.'

The purpose of these revelations is, as always, to stifle argument by pre-made judgement, to strangle any attempt to weigh the issues. Invocations of 'rigid Socialist enclave', 'soviets', 'totalitarianism', do their work; the spectre of the gulag banishes the mild Englishness of what is happening in Walsall; even worse, the reality of what people are suffering there is conjured away – the unemployment rate close to 20 per cent in parts of the town, the poverty of some of the estates, the wasted youth, the decay of the whole reason for existence of the little towns that make up the borough. These things are all thrust out of sight. And, above all, buried in the attacks on the loony left councils, the cabals and conspiracies as they are called (despite the openness of the manifesto and the fact that they won elections), is the defence of the ratepayers: these have become a martyrized, persecuted and impoverished breed. Actually, it is a sentimental euphemism for the rich; one of their many disguises.

But the real storm was reserved for the announcement by Dave Church that the appointments to the Neighbourhood Offices would favour those people who gave evidence of their sympathy with the communities they would be likely to serve, not those who could show the highest qualifications or even local government experience. This was interpreted as meaning political appointments, socialist sympathisers. In fact, the Tribune group was reacting against the theory that council employees carry out the policies of the council, independently of their beliefs; whereas, in fact, the forces of inertia and the structures in place ensure that it is extremely difficult to initiate, to create, to try new departures. The 'existing channels' invite received patterns, the familiar and reassuring tradition of custom and precedent; and even where new policies are carried out these occur with such leaden slowness that those who initiate them will almost certainly be voted out of office before they can be realized; and then they can be accused of failing to carry out their promises. More than this, the very professionalism of the professionals is a source of great conservatism and vested interest: people with secure jobs and high salaries are not best placed to observe the limitations of the structures which they are employed to administer. This is not to attribute malice or inefficiency to such people. It is merely in the nature of things. But any attempt to modify this process – by the appointment of people whose skills were not principally administrative – was bound to provoke the outcry which occurred.

It is interesting to observe how this issue, which at the beginning was seen as a minor local argument, gradually spread, first of all from Walsall into the Birmingham papers, then into the national press, culminating in a sequence of pieces in the *Telegraph* and even a leader in *The Times*.

The local Liberals were reported in the Birmingham papers as describing Labour's appointments policy 'the latest outrage by Walsall's Left-wing Tribune triad'. The Tribune Group,' said a member of the Liberals' Campaign to Liberate Walsall, 'is a ruthless secret society seeking power for itself – irrespective of basic human rights.' Once it had become a question of human rights, there was no limit to the extraordinary inflation of language; and behind Walsall council loomed Poland, Afghanistan, South Africa. 'It is tantamount to the setting up of a Socialist republic in Walsall', 'these sinister happenings', 'the dictatorial world of George Orwell's 1984.' The rhetoric was taken up by national politicians: 'a political witch-hunt' – Tom King, Local Government Minister, July 1980; 'political apartheid' – Norman St John Stevas. Mrs Thatcher herself said, 'If jobs in the public services are to be dependent on the political colour of the applicants, then that would be the end of democracy.' In vain the Labour group responded: 'All we are trying to do is appoint people in the Neighbourhood Offices who have some sensitivity to the social problems of Walsall, socially aware not socialist officers.'

The issue reached the leader column of the *Telegraph* on 26 July 1980. 'Walsall Council Housing Committee has decided that "key jobs" in that department must not go to Conservative supporters. A sub-committee will vet candidates and the chairman will be consulted before any appointments are made. This rule will apply, not only to rising administrators but to girl telephonists. In the deathless and never-to-be-forgotten phrase of the chairman Cllr Dave Church, "O- and A-levels don't really matter there. She would be dealing with working-class people." However less zeal will be used in the appointment of mere rough workmen. To quote

Mr Church again: "We will not be worried about the political viewpoint of a good carpenter. He is a craftsman and that does not matter." The plans of Mr Church are, of course, good, raw, unrefined satire, notions which if dreamt up by some sardonic fellow on a gloomily Conservative newspaper – say the *Daily Telegraph* – might produce a watery smile, but also the comment "Really, that is outrageous. That man goes too far." '

When set against the bleak reality of life for so many people in Blakenall or Goscote, one can only marvel at the way in which an attempt to reach some of those intractable problems – which the Conservative press is far from ignoring when it comes to paying state benefits or law and order or the condition of the family – can be mangled and twisted in such a way as to be denied, obliterated, made *ridiculous*. What it means is that no discussion is permitted on any other terms than those laid down by our masters, the rich and powerful. The means of manipulating and distorting issues are always at their disposal. The trampling of humanity, our constant subordination to the global dictatorship of money, is normal; and any attempt to interfere with it is perverse and unnatural.

But it is a mistake which the left sometimes makes when it attributes all its ills to the media. If the ideology that is implicit in so much reporting on TV and in the press were merely propaganda, then the reality of people's lives would offer a strong corrective to the warping and misshaping of information. But because that ideology is the air we breathe, it colours every aspect of our lives, it has become a substitute for common sense and people are prepared for the kind of onslaught to which Walsall was subjected. The logic of capitalism is the only logic, however aberrant, bizarre and ugly it might be. Capitalism is akin to nature; and anything that runs counter to it is absurd, improper or downright evil. This is how it becomes possible for the *Daily Telegraph* to report with approval (28 July 1980) the idea that employees sympathetic to the problems of the poor would 'infiltrate extreme left-wing socialism into the Authority'.

The way in which socialism becomes a demonic essence, something menacing and abstract that threatens to undermine us, to contaminate all that is good and true, sometimes creates the feeling of what it must have been like to live in the Middle Ages, when the air was full of evil spirits and devils threatening to seize possession of the soul of good Christian folk. The fact that such primitive response can be successfully invoked in this way shows how deep the failure has been to mount any real significant attack on the values and ideology of capitalism, however spectacular all the reforms may appear.

The Times, in those measured cadences that have always been regarded as the last word in authoritative and measured good sense, permitted itself some extraordinary silliness. 'It is an abuse of the council's powers to act in such a way which must inevitably breach its duties and result in a poorer service to the public.' In none of the press coverage was there any mention of a poor and damaged industrial region or of the people who have suffered most from the recession, the cuts in public services, the assault on local autonomy. *The Times* went so far as to offer advice to 'aggrieved ratepayers' and suggested a number of ways in which Walsall council might be brought before the courts; the district auditor might prove the ratepayers weren't getting value for money, certain individual councillors might be held responsible, a charge of maladministration might be brought before the Ombudsman, an individual applicant might sue for damages.

There were other attacks – *Now* magazine, the *News of the World*, the *Sun*; a few more thoughtful pieces – the *Observer*, *Town & Country* Planning in February 1982. But with the actual opening of the Neighbourhood Offices and the speed and efficiency with which this was accomplished, with the immediate and largely favourable reaction of the majority of people in the neighbourhoods, the way in which they released so much energy, the worst of the most destructive press comment subsided. There were still flickerings, of course. Following the large rent increases imposed by government, the arrears of rent in Walsall (as in most other big authorities) rose dramatically. At one point, almost 20,000 of Walsall's 42,000 council house tenants had arrears. The total owed to the council reached £2 million by July 1981. The press attributed this to the policy of decentralization. It was of course, largely caused by the government pressure to increase rents, with the aim of getting as many people as possible to 'choose' to buy their home rather than continue to rent; but with such a proportion of the unemployed, single-parents, large families, the disabled and elderly, pressurizing better-off tenants to buy has the unhappy by-product of increasing hardship for the poorest; for in spite of the possibility of rebates, their sense of failure and exclusion from the mainstream of society is only reinforced.

In the press attacks on the rent arrears, there was no suggestion of the human tragedies that lay behind many of them. Some families I met had arrears of £800 or even £1,000; and, while this is shocking to auditors, the story behind them shows a different perspective. In many ways, the old-fashioned rent collector, whose job was simply to get the cash from the tenants and nothing else, did have an easier job and was more efficient than those who work in the Neighbourhood Offices; because instead of seeing 'defaulters', 'bad payers', you are actually in daily contact with an inescapable story of unhappiness and despair, in the overall picture of which non-payment of rent seems a very secondary issue. Nothing of this ever disturbed the serene and magisterial pages of *The Times* or *Telegraph*: the stories of women struggling to keep their job and their family intact after the husbands had deserted, the woman who was terrorized by her 15-year-old son into giving him money and who threatened to wreck the flat if she didn't. I shall never forget the conversation with one woman in her forties who had continued to work at her factory job even though she knew she had cancer: 'He [her husband] made me go on working because we needed the money. I don't know how much he was getting, he never told me but all I got was £30 a week; so even with the children's allowance, there was never enough money to pay for everything. We'd three children, the oldest was only 10. I didn't tell him at first I was sick. He used to get mad if everything wasn't just as he wanted it when he got home at night; to ask him for more money – it was more than my life was worth. When he knew what was the matter, he got angry. I knew he would. He thought it was my fault.' How much easier it is to create resonant and authoritative phrases in newspaper offices than to try to reach the pain of oppressed and frightened and impoverished people. What the media reaction, the abuse and the misrepresentation, the diversions and the mockery do is keep the lid on that simmering unhappiness and frustration beneath the surface; so that business as usual is maintained, a business that involves drowning out the protests of people until their cries are stifled, their voices smothered, and only the voices of officialdom and authority are heard, the assertions of those who are, as always, the ventriloquist dolls of wealth and power.

7. Neighbourhood Offices: reality and potential

> We deprive people of knowledge. If you ask people how local government works, or how government itself works, they haven't a clue. They don't understand how power works. We deprive people, not by withholding knowledge, not so much by concealing the information, but by placing so many obstacles in people's way, so many diversions and irrelevancies, that people can't find their way through the maze.
> — Brian Powell, leader of Walsall council, 1980–82

The decentralization of housing services was only the beginning of the Labour group's plan to move out many more services into the neighbourhoods. The 33 Neighbourhood Offices were all set up within 12 months, providing rent and all other council payment facilities, council house lettings, repairs and estate management, processing of rent and rate rebates, advice on welfare benefits, the management of some aspects of social services – home helps, meals on wheels; they also acted as a filter, passing on problems to other departments and offering advice on any query brought before them.

A mainframe computer has been used for cash-desk rent and rate information, housing waiting lists and for the position of applicants on those lists, property letting, and the ordering and control of repairs. A microcomputer is used for rent and rate rebates, so that the calculations and processing can all be carried out in the offices themselves.

One of the most exciting things about the scheme is that it operates on many different levels. It fuses practical and efficient delivery of services with a realistic demonstration to people of the benefits and limitations of local government; at the same time, the concentration on where people live offers a focus for community action; indeed, working, as they do, in each particular locality raises all kinds of questions about the idea of community; of living together; of the meaning of fraternity and solidarity.

When Labour lost control in May 1982, the dynamic process of extending and developing the services was immediately curtailed. The plans which were still being formulated to add to the functions of the Neighbourhood Offices still remain, but there is little prospect of them being put into practice while Labour has only a minority representation on the council. There is no reason why certain central government departments should not be decentralized into the Neighbourhood Offices, especially DHSS. There has been some discussion that community policing could be based there; and, in fact, when the Neighbourhood Offices were being defined, they corresponded more closely to police beats than to any other agency's division of the town – wards, social service areas, parishes, etc. There are plans to extend the involvement of social services in the neighbourhood: there is clearly scope for much useful work with families at risk, with those whose job it is to work with them based locally and accessibly. The education welfare office already works in some of the offices, which certainly helps diminish the high truancy rate in some areas, as well as facilitates the administration of school meals, clothing and education grants. The Labour group wanted to negotiate with the gas and electricity boards, with a view to using the offices as a point for paying bills, for reporting defects, to alert the boards to cases of hardship and to avoid cut-offs. There have been ideas about attaching a health component to the offices; a facility which would take some of the pressure off general practitioners by providing certain routine checks.

Although there are already many groups which use the offices for meetings and recreation – pensioners, the unemployed groups, community and tenants' associations, young people's discos –

there is scope for improvement even in the administration of the present services provided by the Neighbourhood Offices. For instance, there should be repair teams based on each office, with yard space for materials. At the moment, the materials are all centralized; a repairs 'caravan' visits each neighbourhood in turn, even though there is a system of emergency repairs, mobile work teams with particular specialities who can be diverted to wherever their skills are needed. It has also been suggested that there should be advisory committees of local people who could take a role in the running of the offices; tenants groups perhaps, local councillors, the recipients and consumers of the services offered in the locality.

'The Neighbourhood Office is really only a building at the moment; and some of those buildings are a bit ordinary – corners of old libraries, halls, prefabs. And some of them are hopelessly cramped. Our building is already overflowing – it can't contain all the activities it could hold. Eventually, the energy and the spirit of the place will spread to the whole neighbourhood. People will say, "Fuck it, why should we put up with that inconvenience, that poor service, that third-rate treatment. We can get together and demand that things are done properly, or some of them we can do ourselves if we're given the resources." That's when it'll take off. The building will become just the office, nerve centre, if you like. But the real transformation has got to be out there, on the estates, in people's homes' (neighbourhood officer).

'There has been some loss of morale since May 1982. Some of the neighbourhood officers thought they saw the writing on the wall and they've gone off to safer Labour areas, where they won't live under the sort of uncertainty we've had to. But this is where it began. This is where it'll all happen again when Labour regains control' (assistant neighbourhood officer).

'There have been inefficiencies. Some days you sit in the office and it seems there's nothing but a sequence of complaints. But that in itself isn't negative: it shows people feel they can complain; there's someone to complain to. That never used to happen. Of course there's always too much work. The years of neglect and indifference are coming back to confront us' (neighbourhood officer).

This view was confirmed by an afternoon I spent in Delves, where whole streets of houses built in the late 1930s are sufffering from subsidence so severe that you can put your hand through the cracks in some of the walls; the floors sloped 'like the crazy house at the fair', as one woman said of her bedroom floor. 'It's the only house in Walsall where you're walking downhill to get into bed.' Windows could not be replaced because the whole structure had shifted, doors had sunk, lavatory and kitchen pipes had become dislocated. One family had been moved out for four months while the repairs to their house were carried out. But they feel that the work wasn't done properly, the cracks merely plastered over, while the structural defects remain. They are living in daily expectation of seeing the cracks reappear, the patches of damp come through. And even to get their house repaired, they had had to go to the Birmingham branch of Shelter. Shelter had carried out an inspection and reported 40 things wrong with the house. The council was taken to court in September 1982 and the magistrates made a Nuisance Order against the local authority. That was when the family were moved out, but they received no compensation for the damage to furniture through damp – clothes, carpets, ward-robes, beds. On the day I visited, they had heard a rumour that some of the houses on the estate were going to be modernized; they were very angry that they should have had four months discomfort, that the work wasn't thoroughly done, when they could have had a proper modernization programme. They were equally angry at the prospect of their house being bypassed in a selective modernization scheme and at the thought of being moved out again while modernization was carried out. 'You can't win. You've got no choice. If you're out of work, what can you do? You're at the mercy of whatever they want to do with you. I can't even withhold my rent if I'm not satisfied, because they stop it at source before I can even touch it. They treat you like children – you're not even fit to handle the benefit you're entitled to.'

It is very difficult for the Neighbourhood Offices to carry out even their limited function at a time when resources are being withheld, when there simply isn't the money to answer the explosion of demand that has been released by providing people with an outlet for the pent-up frustrations and grievances of many years.

In spite of this, the vast majority of the neighbourhood staff are still enthusiastic and committed; even if somewhat sobered by the daily workload. Some of those who had come to Walsall with the idea of transforming the whole structure of local government have had to adjust their aims to the current limitations. 'At least you can try and show people how the system works; but having to administer it at a time of reduced expenditure on housing means that you can easily get identified with old authority figures. People come in, and they see you as the person denying them a house. There's always this tendency to personalize. Because all the big villains have gone away, you can't see the rich, the big capitalists, they assume it must be you. It isn't easy transferring the blame from yourself, sitting there in the office, on to the Thatcher government for housing cuts, or even further on to the manipulators of high finance ... I don't know where they are myself, so how can you expect somebody out of work, never been outside Willenhall, to take on all that?' (neighbourhood officer).

'You do have to show people that you can deliver the service. It's no use being high-falutin about it. People will only support the Neighbourhood Offices because they are seen to offer a better service. People are changed by the results, the evidence. And that's been the achievement. There's no going back now – not because the people are devoted to the Neighbourhood Office idea, but because they have experience of what is possible. That's why even our opponents won't dismantle them now' (neighbourhood officer).

'The trouble is, you work your row out, you deal with a stream of people every day, you see the flaws and failures. Your vision goes. You have to step back and look at the gains. The Labour Party has gained out of it. Ward meetings that used to be two men and a dog have become much more vital, people are more committed, they are beginning to understand the system in a way that they never have before' (assistant neighbourhood officer).

'The Neighbourhoods offer the community the chance to determine its own fate ... to enable people to have faith in their own powers. That means dismantling some of the mystique of the professionals – ask how well have the architects, the planners, the teachers, the social workers served us? Their record is not so hot. People need a little less faith in the experts and a bit more in themselves. You need a system of political education; which, in an indirect way, the Neighbourhood Offices provide' (neighbourhood officer).

'You have a lot of stress. You can see how bureaucratic structures develop: they shield you from some of the stress. The temptation is always there to see the people you are trying to help as the enemy. People sound off at you. You were a twat yesterday, you're a twat today and you'll be a twat tomorrow' (former clerical assistant, now assistant neighbourhood officer).

'People have so little control over their own lives, they're ready to accept other people's interpretation of it. They accept the evaluation of a society that dwarfs and stunts them, and then mocks them for being dwarfed and stunted' (neighbourhood officer).

8. Conclusion

We've accepted the capitalist belief that you can buy happiness
in individual portions, like Kentucky fried chicken. We've been
seduced by the idea that the aim of working-class struggle should
be, not emancipation but wealth. Where we used to share
everything – workplace, streets, beds, toilets, wash-houses,
suffering, pleasure, joys – now you have to buy everything as an
individual. The real sell-out has been persuading us that if we
give up each other, capitalism will reward us individually. All the
commodities that the capitalist system wants to throw at us – the
HP and the debt, the packman and the salesman and the
catalogue – have another side, and that's the worry and the
sorrow, the anxiety and the distrust that goes with them. What
we find we're paying for is the finance houses and the banks and
the profits, wearing ourselves out to get the money, and selling
out friendship and solidarity and neighbourliness into the
bargain – things without price.

— Barry Blower

While people were struggling against appalling working conditions
in the foundries and metal works, it isn't difficult to see how a
sense of shared experience led to the growth of community;
perhaps not quite in the way that occurred in the mining villages or
the cotton towns (there was always too much diversity in the West
Midlands, too many small enterprises for the sort of closeness and
solidarity that developed in single-industry towns). In the West
Midlands, there were always considerable numbers of small

masters who had begun as workmen; there remained ways and means of rising out of the working class that were not possible in mining towns of Yorkshire or the cotton districts of Lancashire. Many of the works were small businesses – harness, metal, leather workshops that were little more than extensions of the houses; and you can still see many of them in the older parts of Walsall. But the fact that it was work, and similar work, that drove people to the inhospitable shelter of the rows of terraced streets clustered around the workplaces meant that there was always a deep sense of the common plight shared by the great majority. The fight for better conditions and wages, improved living standards was always against an identifiable employer, an individual factory-owner from whom redress could be sought. There were always agents and landlords to plead with or hide from when there wasn't enough money to pay the rent; there was the local shop, where strap might be available in the event of sickness or unemployment. And there remained the threat of the workhouse and the pauper's grave to unite people against universal poverty.

What was not foreseen in the struggle by the labour movement for a more secure and dignified life for working people was the possibility that the very basis of the industry which had created these poor and haphazardly built little industrial towns and villages that now make up Walsall might itself one day be seriously eroded. And it is in this context that we have to consider the attempts to regenerate a sense of community – something that was an organic part of the growth of these towns and settlements in the nineteenth-century. In some parts of the area – Darlaston, Willenhall – there are acres of dismantled machinery and rusty metal, twisted girders and heaps of rubble from the bigger factories that developed much later – many of the companies that owed their prosperity to the car industry and which have suffered in the wake of its contraction; many of them firms taken over by multinational companies who have found it more profitable to divest themselves of the machinery and the workers alike. With this intensified disintegration of the whole reason for existence of these older industrial areas, it becomes far more difficult for people to unite than it was against a more tangibly harsh and oppressive system. It is harder to bond together in the face of an *absence* than it is in the direct presence of exploiters and oppressors. When the people who employ us or disemploy us are removed to remote boardrooms in Texas or Osaka, it is far less easy to perceive the ways in which we remain subject to the whim of the market forces which they also serve. It is as though the system has become a great impersonal machine, in which we are all powerless, insignificant figures.

While the old factory boss lived in his neat Victorian villa (or, in Walsall, he was just as likely to live in his shabby dwelling near the works where he could keep an eye on everybody, keeping his money in a greasy cash-box and counting it by candlelight at night), it all seemed so much more straightforward. But when everything depends on vast international transactions of which we can see nothing; when capital, noiseless, winged and infinitely mobile, can withdraw stealthily like a thief in the night and take up its abode in other, more profitable parts of the world, where the working class is more docile and disposed to accept low wages and inferior conditions – there seems to be very few points of contact with it and its agents. It all seems much more powerful; and we are less inclined, because we feel less able, to combat its mysterious and invisible power; even though it rules our lives with the same iron necessity as it did when these towns were thrown up in the wake of the industrial revolution.

But in this absence of immediately identifiable enemies; and in the face of that impersonal system which even the welfare state seems to have become (that great prize won by labour, with its embodiment of the best of the working-class ideal of mutual support and caring); and given the consistent assault on brotherhood and sisterhood, the unrelenting attack on the values and institutions of the working class, it isn't surprising that people have tended to lose their sense of belonging, of cohesiveness and community. It shouldn't surprise us that the migrants from the Third World into the towns readily became identified as the *cause* of that loss of cohesion, even though the recent newcomers to Walsall came in the same migration in search of a better life for themselves and those they love, as the original inhabitants of the town – those who came from Wales and Ireland and the villages of Staffordshire and Shropshire a century and a half ago came on the same quest.

The tendency has been, not for people to intensify their unity and solidarity against these new forces that seem to govern our lives, but to break against them, to turn inwards, to absorb the ideology of capitalism and seek personal salvation. This is done, where possible, by buying our way out, retreating to the suburbs; and, where this isn't possible, by turning away, locking our door against an incomprehensible world, barring the entry to strangers, buying a stronger lock against all the intruders and aliens and muggers and rapists which, the press assures us every day, the world has suddenly become full of.

It is in this context that the Neighbourhood Offices have been set up. That they run counter to the whole temper of the times makes it more difficult for them to succeed. How much harder it is to create a sense of unity, when faced with great indifferent systems, where even a benign idea like 'receiving benefit' sounds like a threat, where immovable functionaries sit behind barred windows and administer bare subsistence, where any kind of labour, no matter how demeaning and degrading, looks like a rescue from the impotence and futility of unemployment. It is so much easier to blame the people we see around us, real flesh and blood with its frailties and weaknesses, than the distant manipulators of our destiny in their remote fortresses. It is so simple to blame the blacks for being here, the young for having it so easy, the old for living too long, the unemployed for being idle, the employed for being greedy; it is even simpler to see a husband as selfish, a wife as indifferent, children as too demanding, parents as too busy, friends as unreliable, comrades as a burden, neighbours as an intrusion; and, in this way, we can see the furthest effects of a brutally damaging individualism into the lives of those who have nothing but their solidarity to fight the assault of capital. We see ourselves as struggling, isolated individuals, pursuing our lonely way through life, panting after all the wonders and promises with which capitalism taunts us and which never seem to go round far enough, which never quite live up to the promise, no matter how much money we may lay our hands on.

It has to be asked whether it is possible to create the kind of unity that is required to fight these forces in our lives; especially since it sometimes seems they are so abstract and beyond our reach, vague and distant shadows. There is no sense in underestimating the work that waits to be done. For it is within a very painful and difficult setting that the people who have set in train the regeneration of neighbourhood have gone to the heart of the way we live now. It is only a beginning; a first and tentative step in the cementing of a solidarity that is the only weapon of those who have nothing but their labour – and their spirit and heart and intelligence – and who are called upon to fight the great global empire which capitalism controls in the declining years of the twentieth century.